COASTAL AND OFFSHORE NAVIGATION

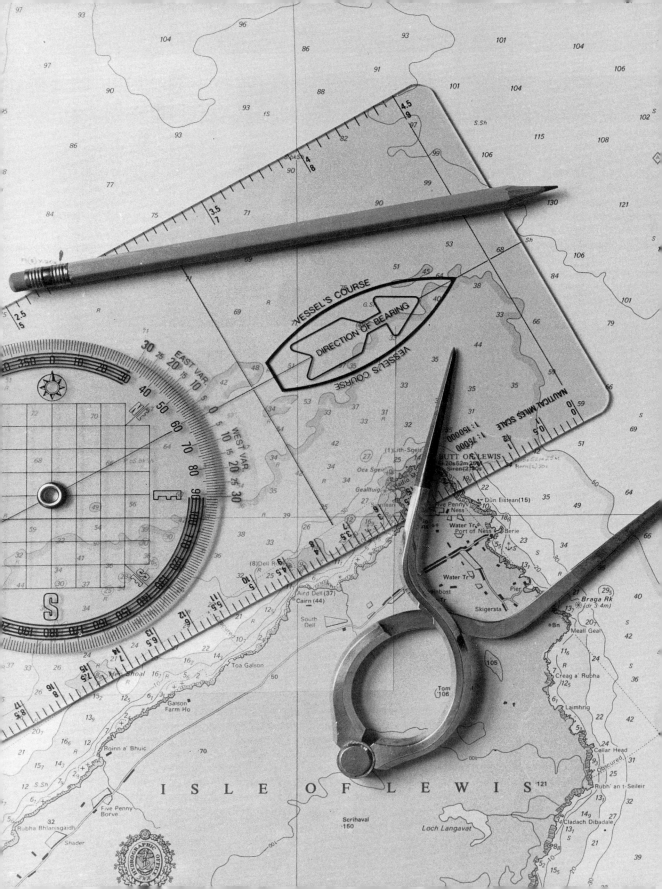

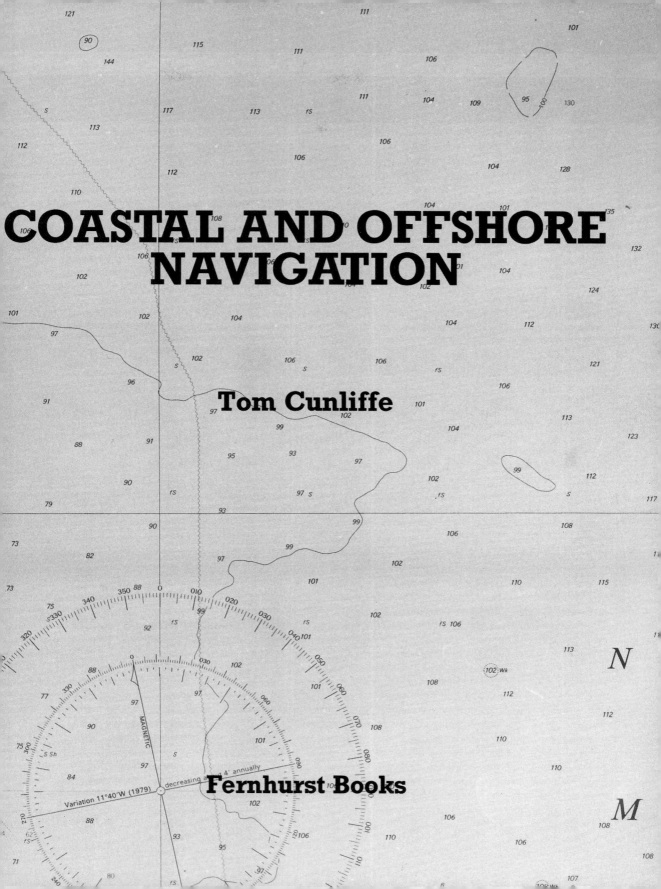

COASTAL AND OFFSHORE NAVIGATION

Tom Cunliffe

Fernhurst Books

First published in 1990 by Fernhurst Books,
31 Church Road, Hove, East Sussex.

ISBN 0-906754-55-0

British Library Cataloguing in Publication Data
Cunliffe, Tom 1947–
    Coastal & offshore navigation.
    1. Coastal waters. Seamanship. Navigation
    I. Title
    823.8929

Printed and bound in Great Britain

Acknowledgements
The author and publishers would like to thank Mike Best and the
Westerly Sea School, Hamble, for the loan of a Westerly Fulmar, and
Chris Wood of Yachtmail, Hamble Point, for the loan of navigational
equipment for the photo sessions. Thanks are also due to Bill
Anderson for his helpful comments on the manuscript.

The Admiralty charts and tidal information reproduced in this book
are Crown Copyright, reproduced from Admiralty charts/publications
with the permission of the Controller of Her Majesty's Stationery
Office.

The portion of Chart c33a on page 10 is reproduced by permission of
the publishers, Imray, Laurie, Norie and Wilson.

The portions of chart NZ 532 are reproduced by permission of the
Hydrographer RNZN.

The information from the Macmillan & Silk Cut Nautical Almanac is
reproduced by permission of Macmillan Publishers Ltd.

Photographs
The photographs on the pages indicated were supplied by the
following individuals or agencies:
Mik Chinery: 61
Tim Hore: 28, 35, 43 (top), 50, 51, 52, 65, 71, 72, 78, 79, 83,
84
Motor Boat & Yachting magazine: 86
Patrick Roach: Cover
John Woodward: 6, 8, 11, 12, 13, 14, 15, 20, 24, 27, 39, 43 (bottom), 45, 66,
76, 77, 94

Edited and designed by John Woodward
Artwork by PanTek, Maidstone
Cover design by Joyce Chester
Composition by Central Southern Typesetters, Hove
Printed by Ebenezer Baylis & Son Ltd, Worcester

Contents

Introduction

The purpose of this book is to give the sailor who has some knowledge of inshore work a solid foundation in the arts of coastal and offshore navigation. The approach to the subject is essentially practical, so that a yachtsman whose seafaring is done in a small sailing vessel can relate to, and profit from, the contents.

Considerable effort has been made to indicate the sort of accuracy that can reasonably be expected in the various facets of small craft navigation, so that the reader can sensibly evaluate his own results.

All the threads with which the navigator weaves his pattern are drawn together at the end of the book in chapters on passage planning and navigational practice. These explain what you actually do, while the earlier chapters give you the knowledge and expertise with which to do it, in reality, out at sea.

1 Charts and Pilot Books

In the long twilight that preceded the general availability of good navigational charts our coastal waters teemed with small craft operated by fishermen. These remarkable seafarers would not have known what to do with an Admiralty chart if you had given them one, yet most of them stayed out of trouble for a lifetime. They did their navigation by using the same rule-of-thumb pilotage tricks that we use today – and a whole lot more we'll never know about. The chart was there all right, but they carried it in their heads.

It did not matter to them, but these fishermen, for the most part, had a very small folio of mental charts. Two, or maybe three, was their lot. Take them a hundred miles from home and send them off to sea and they were in deep trouble.

Today we are lucky. By using readily available charts we can relate what we see above the water to what lies beneath its surface. As a result we are able to perform almost as well as the fishermen, not only on his home ground but anywhere in the world. Charts form the basis of our navigation.

PROJECTIONS

Because charts are printed on conventionally flat pieces of paper and not etched on sections of a sphere representing the globe, there is inevitably some distortion of scale inherent in all of them. The bigger the area covered by the chart, the bigger the distortion. Only if a chart covers an area small enough to be considered flat is there no distortion at all.

Mercator projections

On this type of chart you will notice that all the meridians of longitude are parallel. On a globe, of course, the meridians come together at the poles and only the lines of latitude are parallel.

On a Mercator projection the scale of longitude is constant at all latitudes, while the parallels of latitude are spread further apart the further you are from the equator. This produces some gross distortions of the representation of area in high latitudes. On a Mercator North Atlantic chart, for example, Greenland appears to be the same width, from east to west, as North Africa, whereas in reality it is only one-third as wide.

▷ **On a Mercator chart the lines of longitude are parallel, instead of converging at the poles as they do on a globe. As a result, all the east-west dimensions at or near the poles are 'stretched'.**

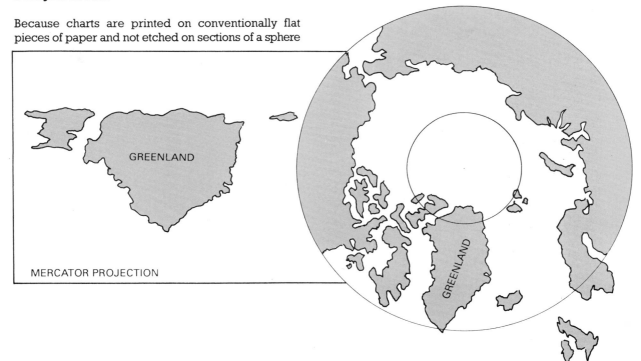

MERCATOR PROJECTION

GREENLAND

GREENLAND

Because of this distortion it is of vital importance when navigating with a Mercator chart that all measurements of *distance* are taken from the scale of *latitude* on the left-hand and right-hand sides of the chart. The *longitude* scale should only be used for defining positions.

Because of the apparent variation in the size of one degree of latitude (or one minute, which represents one nautical mile) as you move towards or away from the equator, it is important to take your measurement from the side of the chart at the same latitude in which you are operating. If you are measuring a distance spanning several degrees of latitude, you should relate your measurements to the mid-latitude of your operation.

▷ **When you are measuring distance on a Mercator chart (top), always use the latitude scale at the side of the sheet (bottom). Note the use of single-handed dividers.**

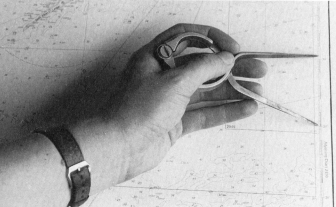

The most beneficial aspect of the Mercator projection is that a straight line drawn between two points will have the same compass heading all the way. This is called a rhumb line, and its use simplifies the navigator's task considerably. For all coastal and offshore work this is what you want from a chart, because ranges and distances are short compared with the size of the Earth. For trans-oceanic distances, however, things are a bit different.

The gnomonic projection

If you simply ruled a rhumb line on a Mercator chart from New York to the Bishop Rock, the distortion of the chart would send you much further than you really need to go.

To make an ocean passage you should ideally be travelling on what is known as a *great circle* route. A great circle is the shortest distance between two points on the surface of a sphere. It is the line described on the surface of a sphere by a plane which passes through its centre (see illustration). It sounds straightforward, but if you draw one on a Mercator chart it doesn't look at all like a rhumb line.

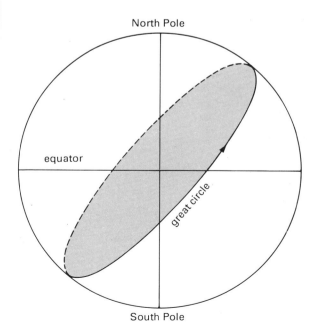

The *gnomonic* ocean chart, however, is projected in such a way that a straight line across it is in fact the great circle course between two points. If you look at the chart illustrated, you'll see that the line crosses each of the converging meridians at a slightly different angle. In practice, in order to stay on this line, you alter course every few degrees (if wind and wave permit, which, in real life, they rarely do).

We have said that coastal charts are Mercator projections, but there is an exception to this rule. *Harbour plans*, with a scale of 1/50,000 or larger, are generally gnomonic projections. Their scales are laid down on the plan itself, and not in the margin.

The reason for using such a projection for these tiny charts is that the gnomonic chart is formed by projecting the Earth's surface from the centre of the globe onto the 'tangent plane' at any convenient point. If the 'convenient point' is the middle of Mevagissy

Harbour and the whole plan is contained by that worthy port, then you can forget about distortions of scale. There aren't going to be any distortions, because the area is so small that the Earth's surface is as good as flat – and the harbour plan will benefit accordingly.

TYPES OF CHART

Admiralty charts are produced in all the different scales required to navigate successfully in British waters. They are available for all foreign waters as well but, in some cases, the locally-produced charts are better for detailed navigation. If you were proposing to visit Norway, for example, you would be well advised to get hold of the Norwegian charts for the area you are intending to sail. Admiralty charts

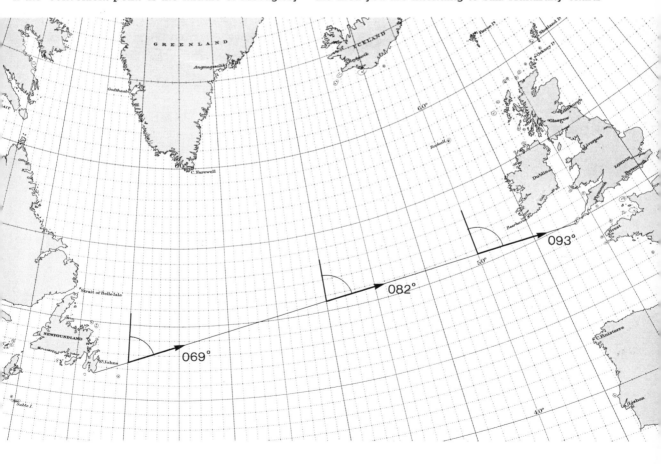

will get you there and take you safely into the main harbours, but not even the Admiralty can produce large-scale charts for all the inlets and anchorages of every coast upon Earth. Be aware of this; if you are going beyond home waters, make suitable enquiries before you leave.

In addition to charts published by the Admiralty there are now many commercially produced charts on the market. These are designed specifically for yachtsmen, and sometimes include additional tidal, passage and pilotage information that can be very helpful. Whether you use these or stick with the official publications is entirely up to you. It is a matter of taste.

⇨ **Part of a 'commercial' chart, designed for small-boat navigation. Compare with the Admiralty charts shown elsewhere in this book, and note the differences in presentation. These charts are folded like road maps, and the resulting creases may make chartwork difficult.**

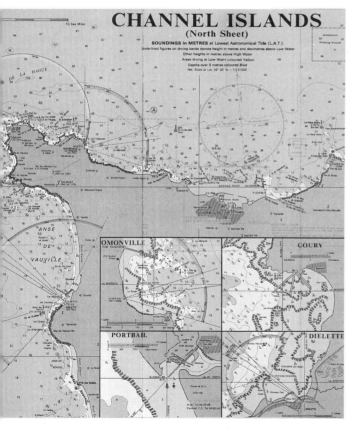

CHART REQUIREMENTS FOR A PASSAGE

Admiralty charts are available in various scales. They range from charts showing the complete North and South Atlantic Oceans on one sheet, down to harbour charts depicting every pile driven into the sea bed. With a selection like this to choose from you should be able to find what you want, but the question often asked is 'What charts do I actually need?'

Since charts are far from cheap nobody wants to buy more than is necessary, but there are few feelings worse than plunging up a narrowing channel with the tide behind you wishing you had bought that last harbour chart instead of last night's bottle of port.

In order to make a coastal voyage the first chart you need is an *overall passage chart*. This should have on it both your departure point and your destination and it is upon this that you will draw up your approximate courses to steer, and work out your passage plan.

If the voyage is going to be a long one you'll find that the detail on your passage chart is insufficient to allow you to plot your progress satisfactorily. If that is the case, you will need a series of *coastal charts* on which to work as you go.

For your arrival you will probably need a *harbour chart* to guide you through the intricacies of the entrance and up to your berth.

If you are intending to pass close to the shore at some point, then make sure you have a chart available that will give you as much detail as you need.

THE ADMIRALTY CHART ATLAS

This most useful publication is available for study at all chart agents, or you can buy one for yourself. If you intend to sail in a lot of different areas, the investment is well worthwhile.

The information is presented as a single line map of the coast. The charts covering it are marked and indexed clearly so that by glancing at the chart atlas you can see immediately which charts you are going to need.

◊ **Three charts for a voyage along the south coast of England from Dartmouth to Poole: an overall passage chart, a coastal chart for the critical area around Portland, and a harbour chart for Poole.**

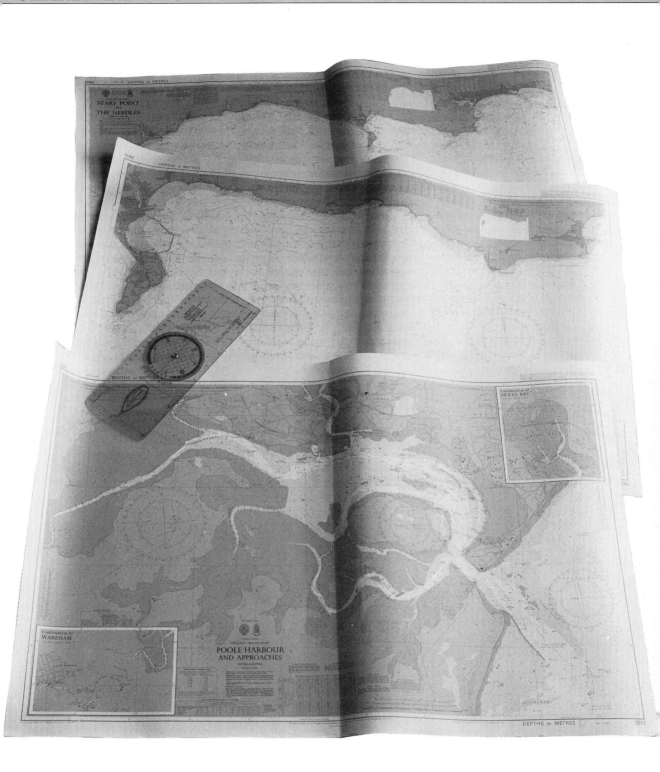

CHART CORRECTIONS

Whether you buy them or borrow them, it is your responsibility to see that your charts are up to date. A new chart from a recognised chart agent will be corrected up to the day of purchase. This is part of the service. Once you walk out the door of the shop you must see to it that your chart remains in this happy state.

Notices to Mariners

Every week the Admiralty publishes a pamphlet entitled *Admiralty Notices to Mariners* in which all the Admiralty charts which require correction are listed and all the details of the corrections given. However, while these might be of great value to a world cruising yacht fully equipped with charts and able to get hold of the *Notices* regularly (a very rare bird indeed), most of the information they contain is of no interest to the home waters yacht navigator.

Being aware of this, and because of the growing numbers of small vessels navigating in home waters, the Admiralty now issues a 'Small Craft' edition of the *Notices* four times a year, concentrated in the summer months. These contain all the information you need to keep up to date any chart from the Gironde to the Elbe. The *Small Craft Notices* do not generally concern themselves with depths greater than seven metres or with other items not considered to be of interest to the operators of small craft.

You can pick up these publications from your local chart agent, but if you prefer, you can arrange for the RYA to send them to you by post.

All chart corrections are referenced by a number for a given year, and the number of the last correction to the same chart is given as well. At the bottom of a properly corrected chart you will find, in the margin at the bottom left-hand corner, a note of each correction as it has been made. By checking the last correction against the reference numbers in the *Notices to Mariners* you can see whether or not the chart is truly up to date.

New editions of charts

Every so often, when the number of corrections on a chart gets out of hand, the Admiralty will issue a New Edition to supersede the old one. The *Notices to Mariners* will advise when this is about to happen.

Navigation Warnings

These are issued daily by Coast Radio Stations, so if you are monitoring your VHF channels, or have a Nav-tex machine, they will keep you right up to date with what is going on in your sea area. Buoys off-station, lights temporarily out of order, dredgers dredging, cable ships to be given a wide berth and so on are all mentioned. The *Notices to Mariners* come by post, but Navigation Warnings are instant, so keep abreast of the latest developments by listening at least once a day.

▽ **Part of a chart obtained from a chart agent, showing a correction. The chart should be up to date when you buy it, but keeping it up to date is your responsibility.**

▽ **Uncharted hazards could spoil your day, and a lot else besides. For advance notice, make a point of listening to the Navigation Warnings broadcast on the radio.**

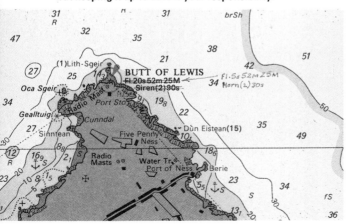

CHART 5011

However much chartwork you have done, sooner or later you'll get caught out by an unusual chart symbol. Chart 5011, which is now a booklet, is an index of all the symbols and abbreviations to be found on Admiralty charts. Every boat should have a copy. Study it carefully on winter evenings, because although many of the symbols appear to be self-explanatory, their meanings are very specific. If your notion of their function is at all hazy you will not be getting proper value from your charts, and they are too expensive not to enjoy to the full.

PLOTTING TOOLS

In order to be able to plot courses, bearings and distances successfully on the chart, you'll need a few simple tools.

The first is a soft, well-sharpened pencil (2B is about right). Pencils need to be soft so that they don't leave a mark on the chart after you have rubbed out a line. It is a false economy to use any old pencil; treat yourself to a box of decent ones. Keep a small knife in a special place. Its sole job is to sharpen your chart table pencils, so clap in irons the man who uses either your sharpening knife or your pencils for anything other than their true purpose.

The second tool is a clean, gentle eraser. Charts are beautiful things. Don't mess them up with a dirty old rubber palmed from your youngest child's pencil case. Keep yours in a safe place.

Dividers for measuring distance off against the *latitude* scale should be as large as you can conveniently handle and, preferably, of the 'one-handed' bow type. It takes very little practice to be able to use them with one hand, leaving the other free to grope for your plotter, your hip-flask, or just simply to hang on.

When it comes to tools for laying off courses and bearings, there are a number of choices available.

Parallel rulers

These are the traditional way of transferring a line from anywhere on the chart to the nearest available compass rose. Unfortunately, in a small yacht, they give rise to a number of difficulties. For example, just as you are making your final 'step' with the rulers, one leg will run into the fiddle on the edge of

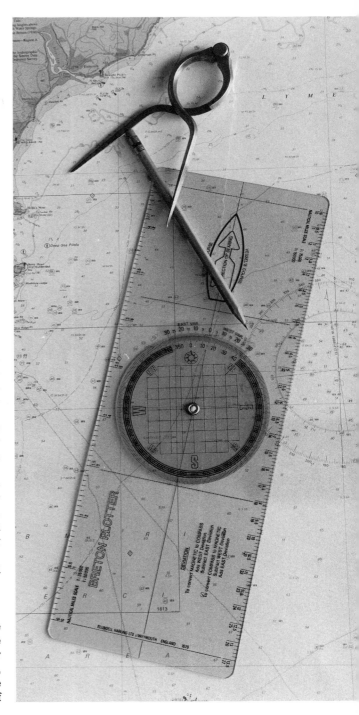

the table, or fall foul of the lead dangling from the RDF set – and you will have to start again. Infuriating on the third successive occasion.

Parallel rulers aren't much good on commercial charts either, because every time you 'step' across one of the many fold lines in the chart, the rules will slip. You don't need this additional aggravation when you are feeling seasick. They also require the use of both hands, but when your yacht is heeled at thirty degrees and bouncing from wave-top to wave-top you need at least one hand to keep you in your seat. All in all, parallel rulers are not much use in a small sailing yacht.

▷ Parallel rulers make use of the compass rose printed on the chart. You align them with your course line (top) and then 'walk' them across to the compass rose to determine the bearing (bottom). It can be a laborious process.

Fortunately these problems are all easily solved by using one of the many plotters on the market. Here are some examples:

Douglas Protractor

Douglas Protractors are the simplest plotters available. They come in large and small sizes and both are very useful indeed. There are two main advantages to the 'Douglas'. There are no moving parts to get stiff, and they have a large-scale lattice of squares that is easily lined up with the grid on the chart.

For some people, the disadvantage of the Douglas Protractor is that it reads only in degrees True.

▷ To use a Douglas Protractor you align the lattice with the grid lines on the chart and read off the bearing from the degree scale round the edge. Simple and sturdy, the 'Douglas' has many applications.

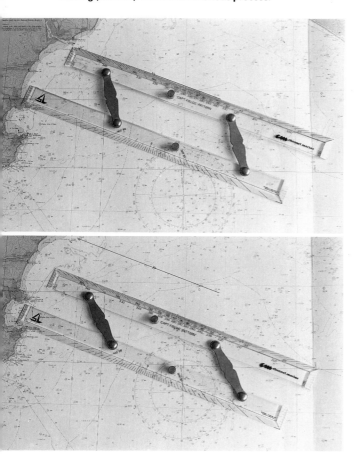

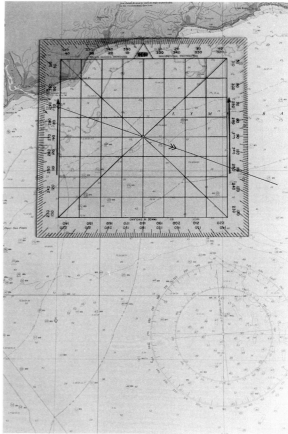

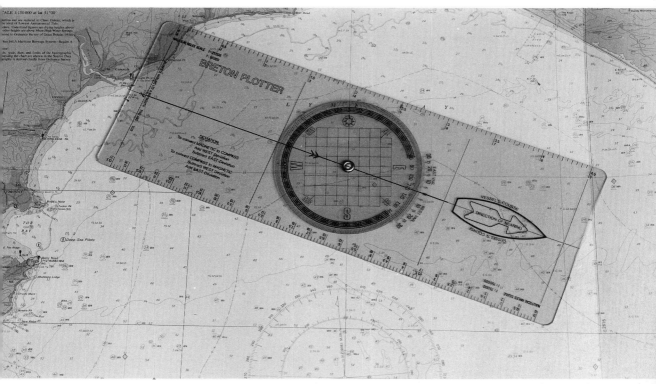

⌒ The Breton Plotter is one of the most effective plotting tools. You lay it along the line, rotate the central disc to align it with the chart grid, and read off the bearing.

Channel Plotter

This tool has the advantage of a longer straight-edge than the Douglas Protractor, and you can set it up to read in degrees Magnetic, if you want to.

There are several plotters which use the same basic system, but the effectiveness of all of them is offset by their fragility. It is only too easy to snap the arm off, although some designs have less fragile arms than others.

Breton Plotter

The Breton Plotter, like the Channel Plotter, can be read in degrees Magnetic, but it has the advantage that without altering any moving parts you can also read the same bearing or course in degrees True, if you want to.

To be set against this, and the low price of the Breton Plotter, is the fact that its grid squares are small. This makes it more difficult to line up accurately.

PILOT BOOKS

The best a chart can ever do is to give you a two-dimensional picture of an area. In order to 'flesh out' the information it gives, you need a Pilot Book.

There are two types of pilot book generally available to yachtsmen. The first is the Admiralty Pilot, and the second is one of the increasingly large variety of yachtsmen's pilots.

The Admiralty Pilot

These rather austere looking volumes are a must for anyone sailing far from home. For descriptions of coastal features in detail they have no equal, so they are a tremendous help when it comes to sorting out one thing from another in an unfamiliar area.

They are rich in material on currents and tidal sets, on inshore passages around difficult headlands, and on general weather patterns. Some of the information they contain is of scant interest to the average yachtsman; you probably do not care that de-ratting can be arranged at your destination! Nevertheless, they do make fascinating reading, and you'll enjoy the odd salty yarn contained within their pages.

The Admiralty's recommendations concerning many of the smaller harbours and inlets can sound rather forbidding. Many a lovely little river is quoted as being suitable for use only by 'small craft' with 'local knowledge'. While these warnings should not be ignored, in many cases they can be treated with a pinch of salt. To find out for certain you should refer to your local *yachtsmen's pilot*.

Yachtsmen's Pilots

These are now available for most of the coasts of Europe. Some are purely commercial publications while others are produced by the members of a yacht club and reprinted for general sale. *The Cruising*

Association Handbook, for example, is a highly worthwhile addition to any yacht's library. The Irish Cruising Club and the Clyde Cruising Club both offer superb pilot books for their respective waters.

A good yachtsmen's pilot book contains not only sailing directions but a lot of useful ancillary information as well. There will usually be sound advice on where to tie up, whether the local yacht club will be pleased to see you, where and how to approach the customs and immigration officers, and very often a vital word on the quality of the launderette.

However, just because a pilot book is offered for sale, this doesn't necessarily mean it is particularly good. Some offer first-class sailing directions but are weak on the 'extras'. Others, lamentably, can tell you all about the beer but are unsound on more important matters. Before you sail to a new area, find a few people who have already been there and ask them about their pilot books. You'll soon build up a picture of which one will suit you.

2 Tidal Heights

Everything you do when sailing in Atlantic waters is influenced by the movement of the tide. It swirls to and fro twice a day, and as it does so it pushes up a tidal surge that varies in height from 0.7 metres at Portland to a mountainous 13.7 metres at equinoctial springs in the Bristol Channel.

If you don't have a solid grip on the technique for working out where the tide stands at a given time, you cannot have any control over the rest of your navigation. As every navigator knows, tidal height, and whether the tide is rising or falling, has a critical effect on the strength and direction of the tidal stream. In the next chapter we'll look into that relationship, but first we'll tackle the matter of how deep the water is going to be.

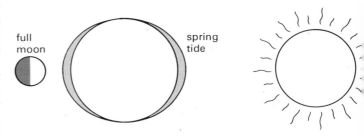

gravity of moon and sun act together

SPRINGS AND NEAPS

Because tides are caused by the gravitational pull of the Moon and the Sun, they are affected by the way one of these is placed in relation to the other.

The Moon goes round the Earth once every 28 days. During this period it is basically in line with the Sun twice: once when it is full and once when it is a new Moon, and invisible because it is between the Sun and the Earth and the side facing towards us is in shadow.

The Moon's effect on the tide is greater than the Sun's, but at times when the two are in line the two gravitional forces act together and sweep up a big tide. These big tides are called *springs* and occur at full Moon and when the Moon is brand new.

When half the Moon is visible it is out of line with the Sun and Earth, so its gravitational field and that of the Sun are working in opposition. This condition produces the small *neap* tides.

This correlation with the lunar cycle explains why spring tides and neap tides both occur twice a month. The name 'spring', in this connection, bears no relationship to the season of the year. It is a coincidence that some of the biggest tides of the year occur around the spring equinox. Similarly large ones turn up in autumn as well, and they are still called 'springs'.

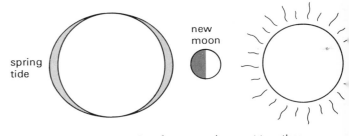

gravity of moon and sun act together

gravity of moon and sun act against each other

You will notice in the diagrams that there are, in fact, two 'tidal surges' going on at the same time on opposite sides of the Earth. The surge on the side away from the Moon is caused by centrifugal force. It is convenient to consider that the Moon is orbiting the relatively stationary Earth, but this is not quite so. What is really going on is that the Moon and the Earth are circling one another around their common centre of gravity. Because this is much closer to the far more massive Earth, it is the Moon which does most of the walking, but nevertheless the Earth is pulled into a rotary motion by this effect.

Because the centre of this motion is the common centre of gravity, which must always lie between Earth and Moon, the centrifugal force affects the opposite side of the globe. The two tidal surges are therefore approximately twelve hours apart.

▷ **Because the Earth and Moon are rotating round a common centre of gravity, centrifugal force causes a tide 'bulge' on the far side of the Earth.**

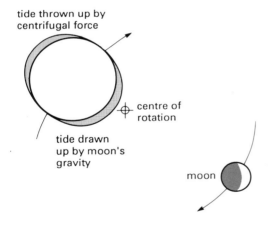

tide thrown up by
centrifugal force

centre of
rotation

tide drawn
up by moon's
gravity

moon

TIDAL HEIGHTS

All depths given on the chart, whether they are soundings or drying heights, are given at the same state of tide. This is the lowest tide that would ever be produced by astronomical effects. It is known as *Lowest Astronomical Tide* (LAT), and is the *Chart Datum*.

Any sounding is a depth below chart datum, while a drying height dries above chart datum. Soundings, you will recall, are the figures in metres and tenths of a metre all over the chart that show the depth of water. A drying height looks like a sounding but is found on a section of the chart coloured green and has a line under it, thus:

Any depth of water to be added to these depths (and there is some, just about all the time) is called the *height of tide*.

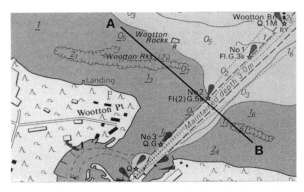

▷ **In this section of a chart the rocks flanking the channel are shown as drying more than two metres above chart datum, while the channel itself is dredged to a sounding of three metres. In practice the water is nearly always deeper than this, as shown in the cross-section below (taken from A to B on the chart). To find the true depth, add the soundings to the height of tide, and subtract the drying heights.**

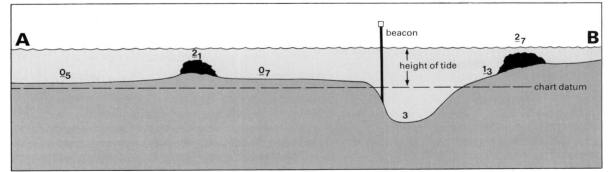

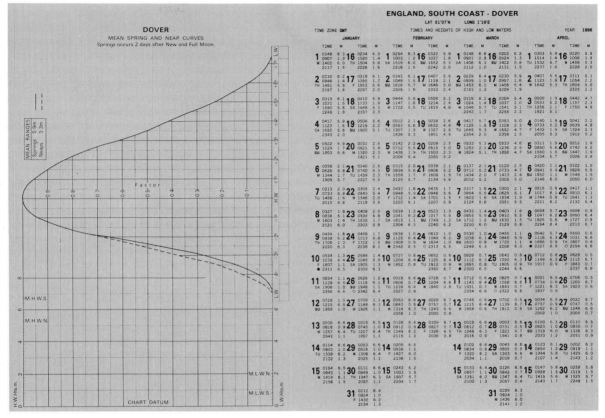

TIDE TABLES AND SECONDARY PORTS

Since the tide times and heights of tides vary between one place and another, most of the major ports of the world carry their own tide tables. These important ports are called Standard Ports. The hundreds of smaller ports which do not have tide tables of their own are known as Secondary Ports, and each one is referred to a particular Standard Port which has similar tidal characteristics. This allows the Admiralty Tide Tables (or your chosen almanac) to be carried around without the aid of a wheelbarrow.

STANDARD PORTS

Illustrated is one of the pages for Dover to be found in the Admiralty Tide Tables. These tables are reproduced in essentially the same form in both the nautical

⌒ The first two pages for Dover in the Admiralty Tide Tables, showing the heights and times of high and low water for each day, and the tidal curve for defining the heights and times of intermediate tides.

almanacs. You will notice that close to the top of the tidal curve is a box showing the mean ranges of spring and neap tides.

MEAN RANGES	
Springs	5·9m
Neaps	3·3m

The *range* of a tide is the amount by which that particular tide will rise or fall; in other words, it is the difference between high and low water. The *mean range* is simply an arbitrary range which represents an average spring or neap tide.

By inspecting the tide tables for the day in question and comparing the range with the mean ranges given, you can see at a glance whether a tide is a spring, a neap, or something in between.

Example Thursday 27th March, morning tide. What is the range?

High water	6.7m
Low water	0.5m
Range	6.2m

This is clearly a spring tide as the mean spring range is given as 5.9m.

The heights of tide given in the tables are heights *above Chart Datum*, so they are always added to the soundings on the chart. If the charted 'depth' is a drying height, then it may or may not be covered at low water. In some cases, high water may not quite cover it either.

TIME ZONES

All tide tables for Britain give their times in Greenwich Mean Time (GMT). It is a good idea when dealing with tides for British waters to keep all your calculations in GMT. Label them as such until you come up with your final answer, and then add an hour, if necessary, to convert the final answer to local time. If you don't do this, you will find that some of your Secondary Port calculations are not as accurate as they could be. Remember that in summer the pubs may shut at 2130 GMT, so a mistake works against you and you may suffer a mutiny in consequence.

For the convenience of everybody the world is divided up into 24 time zones, one for each hour of the sun's progress 'around the world'. These zones (which, incidentally, each cover 15° of longitude) are numbered east and west of Greenwich, and are designated −0100, −0200 etc. If they are to the eastward and +0100, +0200 and so on to the westward. Since many of the European countries, including France, are in a different time zone from Britain it is important to know how to cope with this.

Here is how it works. The time zone (either GMT, or −0100, +0100 etc) is shown at the top left-hand corner of the page in the tide tables. If you are in time zone −0100 you simply subtract one hour from the time given in the tide tables to convert the time to GMT. If in zone +0100, you add an hour.

Example High water Cherbourg is at 1400 Zone Time. Convert to GMT.

Local time	1400
Time zone	−0100
GMT	1300

So high water Cherbourg is at 1300 GMT.

Always be sure to check your time zone for Continental ports. Many a bad mistake has been made by getting it wrong, or forgetting it altogether.

Just as you work in GMT and convert the final answer, if necessary, to BST when in home waters, when you are in a different time zone you should produce all your working in the zone time of the country concerned, and then make any corrections for 'standard' or 'summer' time at the end of the calculation.

HIGH AND LOW WATER AT SECONDARY PORTS

The illustration shows the way one almanac sets out the information for calculating tides at secondary ports. Others set it out differently but the principle is essentially the same.

TORQUAY 10-1-21
Devon

CHARTS
Admiralty 26, 1613; Stanford 12; Imray C5, Y43; OS 202
TIDES
−0500 Dover; ML 2.9; Duration 0640; Zone 0 (GMT).

Standard Port DEVONPORT (⟵)

Times				Height (metres)			
HW		LW		MHWS	MHWN	MLWN	MLWS
0100	0600	0100	0600	5.5	4.4	2.2	0.8
1300	1800	1300	1800				

Differences TORQUAY

+0025	+0045	+0010	0000	−0.6	−0.7	−0.2	−0.1

You will see that various times of high and low water at the standard port are given, while the height differences are given for mean high water springs, (MHWS), mean high water neaps (MHWN) etc.

The time differences are quite simple to operate. If high water at Devonport is at 0100 or 1300, you add +0025 – or 25 minutes – to it; this gives you the time at Torquay. If high water was at 0600 or 1800 you would have to add 45 minutes. The same applies to low water.

If high water or low water at Devonport falls between the times given, you interpolate. Usually this can be done in your head, but if you have a particularly awkward one you may choose to write it down. Sometimes you will have to interpolate the height differences as well. For example, suppose high water Devonport is at 0330. What time is high water at Torquay? Since 0330 is halfway between 0100 and 0600, the tidal difference will be halfway between +0025 and +0045, which is +0035.

Since you need to remember the time and height of high and low water at the secondary port, it pays to write the whole thing down.

Example What is the time and height of high and low water on the morning tide at Torquay on 23rd October? The working is shown below.

STANDARD PORT: *DEVONPORT*

LOW WATER

Time	Height
0215 GMT	1.6m

HIGH WATER

Time	Height	Range
0809 GMT	5.1m	3.5m (halfway between spring & neap)

DIFFERENCES: *TORQUAY*

+0008   −0.2   +0039   −0.7

| 0223 GMT | 1.4m | 0848 GMT | 4.4m | 3.0m |

21	0119	1.1
	0715	5.4
TU	1334	1.2
	1927	5.3

22	0147	1.4
	0740	5.3
W	1403	1.4
	1955	5.0

(23)	0215	1.6
	0809	5.1
TH	1433	1.7
	2027	4.7

24	0243	1.9
	0844	4.8
F	1506	2.0
	2107	4.4

MEAN RANGES	
Springs	4·7m
Neaps	2·2m

HEIGHTS BETWEEN HIGH AND LOW WATER

Because there are 24 hours in a day and high and low water happen only twice each, for most of the time the tide is at a height somewhere between the two. For years the business of working out how much water the tide is actually supplying caused consternation amongst part-time navigators. Not any more. The Hydrographer of the Navy has solved the problem.

If you look at the Admiralty Tide Tables you will find that each set of tables is accompanied by a tidal curve superimposed on a lattice of squares. Each Standard Port has a curve to suit its tidal characteristics. Using these curves will solve all your tidal height problems with amazing simplicity, as the following examples will make clear.

There are two basic questions you will be asking about tide heights: what *time* will there be a given height of tide? What will the *height of tide* be at a given time? The easiest way to explain how you find the answers to these questions is to give an example.

JANUARY					
	TIME	M		TIME	M
1	0148	6.3	**16**	0234	6.3
	0907	1.3		1020	1.4
W	1402	6.0	TH	1504	5.8
	2117	1.5		2226	1.8
2	0230	6.2	**17**	0319	6.1
	0946	1.4		1055	1.7
TH	1451	5.9	F	1553	5.6
	2157	1.6		2257	2.0
3	0319	6.1	**18**	0410	5.9
	1031	1.5		1133	1.9
F	1550	5.8	SA	1649	5.3
	2245	1.8		2337	2.3

Example What time (around lunchtime) will the tide in Dover harbour have achieved a height of 4.7 metres on 1 January? The relevant section of the Dover tide table is illustrated above, while the curve (filled in) is shown below. The method is as follows:

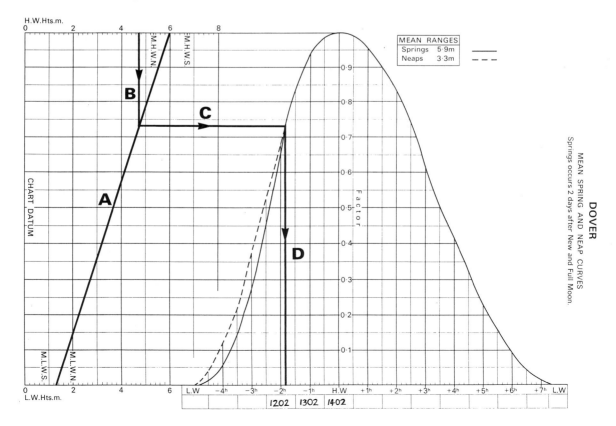

1 Note down the time and height of low and high water:

0907 GMT 1.3
1402 GMT 6.0

RANGE is 4.7 metres: halfway between spring and neap

2 Draw a line A which joins low water, at the bottom of the lattice, with high water at the top.
3 Enter the times of high water and a few hours before in the time boxes beneath the curve.
4 Drop a line from a point at the top of the lattice where the value of the tide is 4.7 metres (line B) to meet the diagonal line A.
5 Draw a line across the lattice (line C) as far as the 'tide rising' curve. Notice that there are two curves, one for spring tides (solid) and one for neap tides (pecked). Sometimes you'll have to interpolate between them, but in this case they coincide.
6 Drop a line (line D) down to the time boxes from the curve and read off the time. In this case it is about 1215 GMT, and that is the answer to the question.

You can see that if you were asking what the height of tide would be at 1215 GMT, you would simply use the system the other way round by starting with the time box and working, by way of lines D, C and B, back to the tidal height at the lattice end of the diagram. Either way, you always begin by drawing in the diagonal A.

If you want to know at what time the tide will have *fallen* to a certain height, you would carry line C across to the right-hand side of the curve where the tide is falling, and drop line D down from that point.

Note that the answers given by these curves are the *total height of tide*. You do *not* have to add the height of low water to your answer, as with some of the older methods. To find the depth of water, you simply enter the curve, as above, and add your answer to the sounding given on the chart. It is that easy.

The Solent area

Because of the eccentric nature of the tidal streams around the Isle of Wight, the Solent ports and those adjacent experience an extra long high-water stand. This makes the exact time of high water almost impossible to predict , so the tidal curves for all the secondary ports in the Solent area (from Swanage to Selsey Bill) operate from low water instead of high water.

This apart, there is no difference in using them, except that in some cases a curve is supplied not only for mean springs and mean neaps, but also for a tide in between. This is because the spring and neap curves vary so much that interpolation is impossible. Where there is one of these extra curves you should interpolate between it and either the spring or neap curve, as necessary.

▷ Some areas such as the Solent on the south coast of England have eccentric tidal patterns caused by tidal streams swirling round islands. In the case of the Solent, low water is much more predictable than high water, and forms the basis of the Admiralty tidal curve.

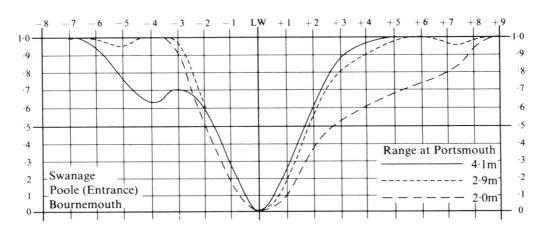

Range at Portsmouth
———————— 4·1m
– – – – – – – 2·9m
— – — – — 2·0m

Swanage
Poole (Entrance)
Bournemouth

EXPECTATIONS OF ACCURACY

While you should always make every effort to get your calculations right, it is vital to understand that since nature has not heard of tide tables or computers the tidal predictions may not always be perfectly accurate. The height of tide is affected by barometric pressure at the rate of 0.15 metres for every 17 milli-bars either side of 1017. If the pressure is high, the levels of high and low water are depressed. Low pressure encourages a higher level. Levels are also disturbed by onshore or offshore winds. A gale out by the Azores that you know nothing about may well upset your careful working. The best way to deal with these uncertainties is to hope for the best, but prepare for the worst. Operate from a position of strength – a properly worked calculation – and then apply a margin of safety to the figure you have reached.

DEPTH IN PERSPECTIVE

When you are deciding how much water you will need to negotiate a passage, what time a bank will dry, when you will take the ground, or almost any other problem involving tidal height, you should always allow a good *margin for safety*. You are not playing a game, or doing an academic exercise where a wrong answer brings your marks down a little. We are talking here about grounding your ship. Hitting the sand spoils your day, and could give the insurance companies (including the life insurance companies) plenty of paying out to do.

How much margin you leave will depend on circumstances, but you should be taking into account such things as:

- Waves on a bar
- Tide rising or falling (will you float off?)
- Bottom soft or hard (a gentle slowing down or a terminal BANG)
- Are you certain of the information on the chart? (shifting sands on bars)
- Are you sure of your interpolation?
- What about the weather, what accuracy can you expect? Will the tide behave itself?

▽ Your tidal calculations may be impeccable, but you must always allow a margin for safety. Getting stranded may not wreck your boat, but it will certainly spoil your day.

DEPTH DIAGRAMS

When working any tidal height question a diagram on your rough working pad helps to crystallise the mind.

Example 1 What time will I dry out alongside this berth? I have a depth of 2.7 metres on my echo sounder at the moment, and my draught is 1.9 metres.

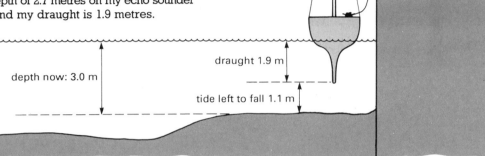

depth now: 3.0 m

draught 1.9 m

tide left to fall 1.1 m

Note that the echo sounder is *below* the surface of the water, so is reading, on this particular boat, 0.3 metres *less* than the actual depth. Measure your own transducer depth, and deal accordingly, unless you have a sounder of the type that is adjustable. These wonderful devices can be calibrated to read the true depth of the water.

Since you know the state of tide now from your tables, solving this problem is simply a matter of using the curve to see when there will be 1.1 metres less water.

Example 2 At what time will the tide have risen sufficiently for me to cross the bar at Gasworks Creek? I draw 1.9 metres and I would like one metre of clearance. The bar dries 0.6 metres.

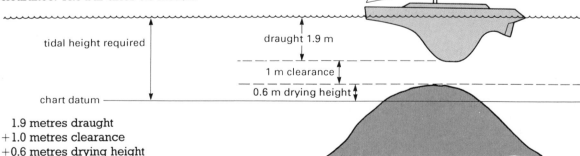

tidal height required

draught 1.9 m

1 m clearance

0.6 m drying height

chart datum

  1.9 metres draught
+1.0 metres clearance
+0.6 metres drying height

=3.5 metres height of tide required

Enter the curve, and find out when you will have it.

Example 3 *Reduction to soundings.* I am sailing along and I want to use my echo sounder to see if I am near a particular line of soundings. I know what time it is.

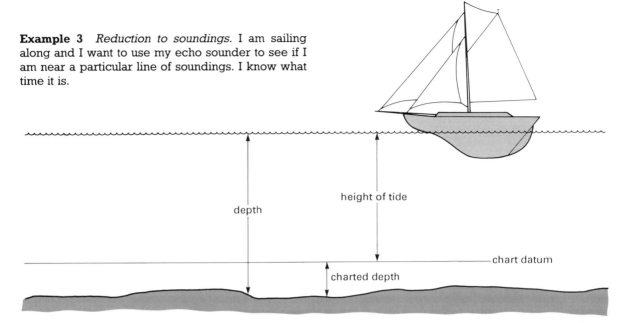

depth

height of tide

chart datum

charted depth

If the depths are great, you will probably ignore the small corrections for your echo sounder here. Common sense will dictate the wisdom of this.

In this case the charted depth added to the height of tide will give you the depth on the echo sounder. So if you work out the height of tide from the curve and subtract it from the depth on the sounder you will have reduced the depth to soundings.

As you can see, a simple picture can save a lot of brain twisting. Set yourself some practical problems, draw the diagrams and get used to the concepts. Then when you need to work things out in a hurry, you'll have the satisfaction of doing it like a well-oiled machine.

3 Tidal Streams

Tides do not only make the water level rise and fall; they also make the water flow to and fro. These *tidal streams* can often be very powerful, and it is essential that you take account of them in your navigation.

RIVERS AND SMALL ESTUARIES

The tidal stream in a river or estuary usually behaves exactly as you would expect. It floods into the river until the time of high water, stands at high water for a short while and then ebbs away to the sea once more until the time of low water.

The rate of the stream varies according to the river, but usually it begins slowly in the first hour, builds up to a maximum in the third and fourth hours and then dwindles off to slack again, both ebbing and flooding. In general, the ebb tide in a river is more powerful than the flood tide because the river is, after all, trying to flow to the sea. When the tide ebbs it adds to the river's natural tendency. When it is flooding the tide is 'backing the river up' and so it flows more slowly.

COASTAL AND OFFSHORE STREAMS

Like streams in rivers, tides along the coast and off-shore also conform to a 12-hour cycle. The difference is that their directions are not normally to and fro and their times of change do not necessarily coincide with the times of high and low water at coastal ports. Slack water at Dover, for example, occurs about 1½ hours before high water and 4½ hours after high water. At the time of high water the tide in the offing may well be streaming past at two knots.

SHALLOW WATER EFFECTS

All currents flow faster in deep water than in shallow, and tidal streams are no exception to this. If you find yourself having to sail against the tide in a river, stay as close to the bank as you dare. If you are coming along the coast creep in towards the beach, if you can. It will make a lot of difference to your progress.

⇨ The tidal stream is nearly always weaker near the beach, so it pays to hug the coast when fighting a foul tide.

⌂ **Keep an eye open for local tidal conditions. The water swirling round a buoy will indicate the turn of the tide more accurately than the tidal atlas.**

THE TIDAL STREAM ATLASES

The streams around our shores are predictable, and are set out very clearly in the Admiralty tidal stream atlases. If you don't want to brass up for these you will find them reprinted in a shrunken but still intelligible form in your nautical almanac.

Each page of a tidal stream atlas refers to a one-hour period and is referenced to the time of high water at the most convenient Standard Port.

Illustrated is the page for five hours after high water Portsmouth from the 'Solent and Adjacent Waters' tidal stream atlas. The great joy of using tidal information presented in this way is that you can see at a glance what the overall tidal picture is. In this case the tide off the southern tip of the Isle of Wight is ebbing while the flood has begun in the Solent. The figures represent the velocity of the stream, the larger being the spring rate and the smaller representing the neap. For clarity the decimal points are left out so that in this case the tide off Cowes is 0.4 knots at neaps, and 0.8 at springs.

You can normally do any necessary interpolation by eye, but if you want to be very accurate, there is a simple diagram for interpolating rates on the back of the atlas.

◊ **A page from an Admiralty tidal stream atlas.**

▽ **The information as published in Macmillan's Almanac.**

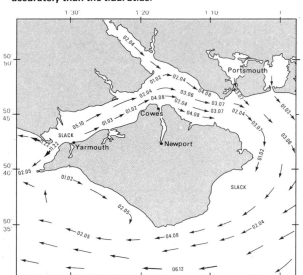

5 Hours after HW Portsmouth (0515 after HW Dover)

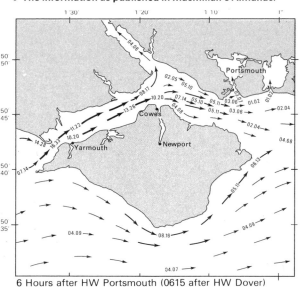

6 Hours after HW Portsmouth (0615 after HW Dover)

CAUTION:— Due to the very strong rates of the tidal streams in
some of the areas covered by this Atlas, many eddies may occur.
Where possible some indication of these eddies has been included.
In many areas there is either insufficient information or the eddies
are unstable.

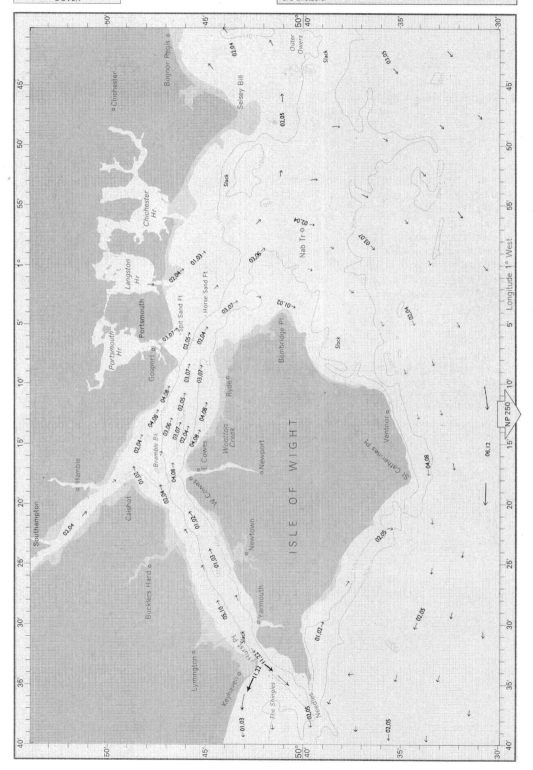

TIDAL DIAMONDS

An alternative source of information concerning tidal streams is available on the chart. You will have noticed magenta diamonds each containing a capital letter at various locations on Admiralty charts.

These are locations of reference for tidal stream information. Somwhere near the edge of the chart you will find a small table set out, with a column of figures for each tidal diamond. You will see that for each hour before or after high water at a standard port the spring and neap stream rate is given, and its direction.

This information is accurately presented, and if you are close by a diamond it is of the utmost value. If you are in between two or three tidal diamonds, or passing from one to another, you will need to inter-polate with great circumspection to approximate to a good result.

Bear this in mind, and use both your diamonds and your atlas as needs must and as common sense dictates.

○ **Tidal diamonds are usually few and far between, but this section of chart has three. The relevant tidal information appears in a table at the edge of the chart (reproduced below) with a key (below left).**

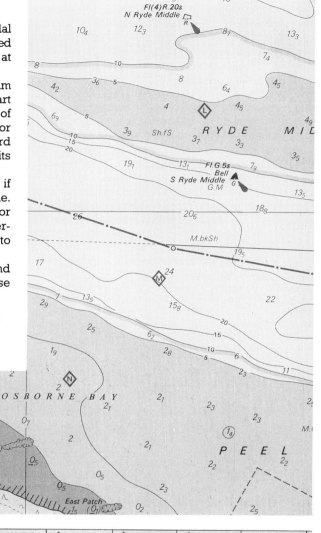

Hours	Geographical Position	◇K 50°46'8N 1 13·8W			◇L 50°46'3N 1 14·2W			◇M 50°45'8N 1 14·4W			◇N 50°45'5N 1 14·8W			◇P 50°48'3N 1 15·3W			◇Q 50°46'5N 1 17·5W			◇R 50°48'4N 1 17·5W		
Before High Water 6	Directions of streams (degrees) / Rates at spring tides (knots) / Rates at neap tides (knots)	–6	112	1·7 0·8	107	1·6 0·8	119	1·3 0·6	137	0·9 0·4	110	0·7 0·4	084	2·5 1·2	022	1·8 0·9
5		–5	106	2·0 1·0	118	1·4 0·8	116	1·9 1·0	144	0·8 0·4	101	1·1 0·5	090	2·7 1·3	038	1·0 0·5
4		–4	100	1·9 1·0	123	1·4 0·7	115	2·0 1·0	144	0·7 0·3	100	1·1 0·5	091	2·7 1·4	070	0·4 0·2
3		–3	096	1·4 0·7	121	1·0 0·5	116	1·2 0·6	147	0·3 0·1	093	0·4 0·2	090	2·2 1·1	058	0·4 0·2
2		–2	086	0·4 0·2	071	0·1 0·1	124	0·3 0·2	298	0·4 0·2	303	0·3 0·1	096	0·9 0·4	019	1·4 0·7
1		–1	286	0·6 0·3	300	0·8 0·4	285	0·7 0·3	307	1·0 0·5	296	1·0 0·5	259	0·7 0·3	008	0·5 0·2
High Water 0		0	283	1·6 0·8	295	1·9 1·0	294	1·8 0·9	311	1·4 0·7	293	1·3 0·6	267	2·8 1·4	232	1·0 0·5
After High Water 1		+1	285	2·3 1·2	288	2·1 1·0	293	2·4 1·2	312	1·3 0·6	290	1·2 0·6	268	3·8 1·9	230	1·1 0·5
2		+2	287	2·4 1·2	290	1·3 0·7	295	1·8 0·9	321	0·7 0·4	283	0·8 0·4	269	3·0 1·5	226	1·2 0·6
3		+3	286	1·4 0·7	296	0·2 0·1	317	0·6 0·3	082	0·2 0·1	191	0·4 0·2	269	1·8 0·9	205	1·4 0·7
4		+4	270	0·4 0·2	099	0·3 0·2		0·0 0·0	122	0·7 0·3	139	0·8 0·4	275	0·5 0·2	180	2·4 1·2
5		+5	120	0·6 0·3	099	0·7 0·4	115	0·4 0·2	124	0·8 0·4	107	0·4 0·2	083	0·8 0·4	070	0·2 0·1
6		+6	113	1·4 0·7	101	1·4 0·6	120	1·0 0·5	130	0·8 0·4	105	0·5 0·2	084	2·0 1·0	025	1·6 0·8

THE 'TIDAL HOUR'

Notice that in both presentations of tidal stream values, the reference is to high water at a standard port, or to so many hours before or after high water.

Suppose you are interested in two hours before high water. The information you are given is what is *actually happening at that time*. It doesn't begin then!

For navigation purposes you should assume that the tide does what is predicted for a whole hour and then suddenly changes to the next hour's predictions. If you do this over a period of several hours, the obvious nonsenses cancel one another out and your results are generally quite good. Nevertheless you must remember that the hour's prediction begins half an hour before 'two hours before High Water', and ends half an hour after.

⬑ The designated times given in tidal information occur halfway through 'tidal hours'. For most purposes you can assume that the tidal rates and directions change abruptly at the end of each tidal hour, although this is obviously not so in reality.

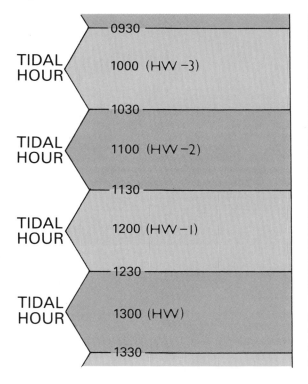

TIDE-INDUCED EFFECTS

When imagining dangerous seas a landsman will usually conjure up a vision of a heroic barque fighting a tempest in deep water, while her honest mariners cling in despair to the rigging, the wheel and each other.

The facts, as usual, are at variance with popular conceptions. The worst seas of all are generally encountered near land, where there is a strong tidal stream operating in conditions that do not encourage it to flow smoothly.

The simplest case of this is a weather-going tide. When the tide is running downwind it has a smoothing effect upon the sea, but when it turns and begins churning its way to windward it piles up short, steep, breaking seas.If a strong tide is flowing through a confined channel the effects can be dramatic. You are well advised to take heed of this when deciding where to go, and when.

If you see symbols like these on the chart, then look out for trouble, especially when the tide runs to windward.

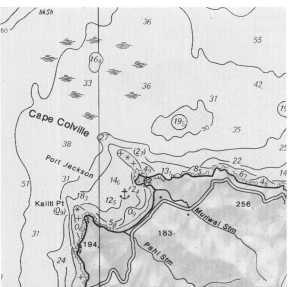

Shallow areas are often bad news. You may find that the seas break even in calm weather as the tide boils over a shoal that stands in otherwise deep water. In a gale the place will turn into a deathtrap.

When two conflicting tidal streams meet you may experience overfalls (steep, broken waves). This effect often occurs off headlands and is aggravated if the bottom is uneven. Headlands like these are notorious for the number of vessels that have foundered in their tidal races. Few small craft can survive the Race of Portland in a south-westerly gale.

Whenever you are in any doubt you should give a major headland a wide berth. The chart will help you to decide how far off you should pass, but do not forget to study your pilot books. Occasionally they will advise of an inside passage, slipping through between the cliff and the overfalls. In fair weather this can be quite illuminating, but do not attempt such a course of action in bad conditions unless you have real local knowledge and are sure of your ground. Once in a while you will find that an 'inside passage' has ceased to exist for a tide's duration and, having committed yourself to it, you will be confronted by wall-to-wall breakers. If you see this coming you are in for a very bad time indeed so batten down, clip on and make peace with your Maker. If it isn't your day to go, He'll see you through so that you will know better next time!

▱ **The Race of Portland is a notorious deathtrap for small vessels. The danger is indicated on the chart, but for the true picture you must consult the tidal stream atlas. The inset section shows how the tide squeezes past the headland and swirls back on itself to create the race just off the point. The area between the point and the race itself is the 'inside passage'.**

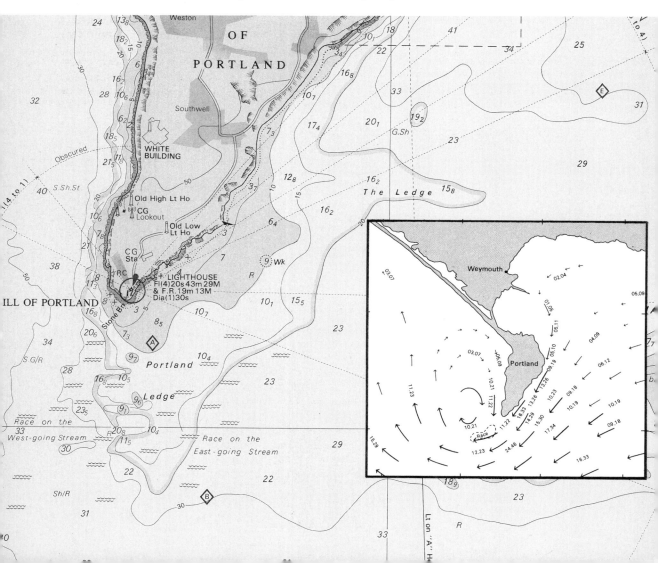

4 The Steering Compass

The three primary sources of input to the navigator are the depth sounder, the log and the compass. Of these the most important is the compass. If you have no visible reference points to refer to, you are lost if you don't have one.

Unfortunately, although it is the most vital piece of navigational equipment you possess, it is also the most prone to interference and inaccuracy. These problems are of two types: *variation*, which is the changing difference between true and magnetic north, and *deviation*, which is compass inaccuracy caused by features inherent in the boat herself.

VARIATION

True north lies in the direction of the geographic pole which is the position of the Earth's axis in the Arctic Ocean. All the meridians converge upon the North Pole and it is a precise point.

The magnetic pole wanders slowly around the frozen north and, at the time of writing, is enjoying a position somewhere at the north end of the Canadian Arctic archipelago. The difference between the true and magnetic pole creates a compass error which alters according to your location. In Europe, for example, compasses show an error to the west of true north. The number of degrees by which the two differ is called the *variation*.

The variation for a particular area is shown on charts on the east-west line of the compass rose; sometimes a magnetic rose is shown as well, for the convenience of the navigator. Notice that the variation is constantly changing, so if your chart is of great antiquity you may have to add or subtract a degree from that stated.

Whether you plot in degrees True or degrees Magnetic is entirely up to you, but *don't forget which you are using*. Always write the letter 'T' or 'M' after a course or bearing just to remind yourself.

⇩ A compass rose on a chart, showing the magnetic variation for the area, and an inner magnetic rose.

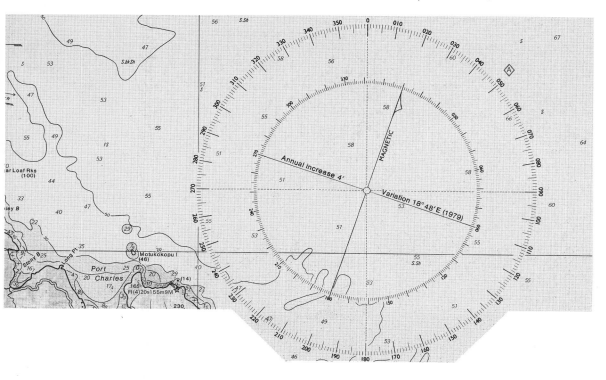

Converting between magnetic and true

You will often find it necessary to convert degrees Magnetic to degrees True, and vice versa. As with many such navigational problems, the easiest way to get this one right every time is with a diagram. Suppose the variation for an area is eight degrees west, and you have a course of 187 degrees True to take up to the compass.

First draw a rough diagram of a blank compass rose with true north indicated.

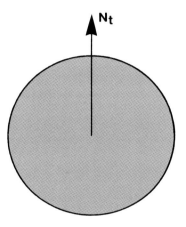

Then draw in magnetic north, eight degrees to the westward of true north.

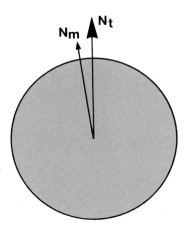

Now draw in the direction of the course or bearing.

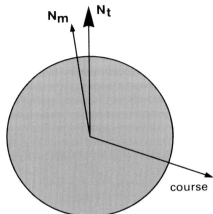

You can see immediately that the angle between the course and magnetic north is greater than the angle between the course and true north, so in this case you must clearly *add* the variation. *If the variation is to the west, the compass bearing has a higher value than the true bearing.* In other words: ERROR WEST, COMPASS BEST (biggest).

Now suppose the variation were to the east. Draw another diagram and you will notice straight away that the angle between the magnetic north and the course is *less* than that between the course and true north. This means that you must *subtract* the variation. *If the variation is to the east, the compass bearing has a lower value than the true bearing.* In other words: ERROR EAST, COMPASS LEAST.

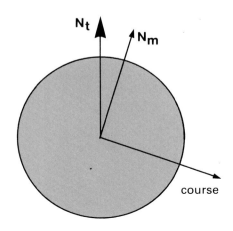

DEVIATION

Correcting for variation will compensate for the vagaries of magnetic north, but will take no account of the vagaries of your own compass. Collectively known as deviation, these errors can be caused by any pieces of magnetically active metal that are near enough to the compass to interfere with its function. Deviation will vary with the ship's heading because the position of the lumps of iron causing it will vary relative to the north pointer on the compass card, as the boat turns 'under' the compass.

Deviation, for a given heading, is expressed as the number of degrees of error that the compass reads east or west of the actual *magnetic* ship's heading.

○ In this boat the engine is causing compass deviation. As the heading changes, the position of the engine changes too, dragging the compass needle with it.

The compass adjuster
The best way to deal with deviation is to have a compass adjuster work his magic. Many modern compasses, particularly of the 'bubble' type, contain tiny bar magnets which can be rearranged to compensate for deviation. This is a skilled job, but a good compass adjuster will accomplish it in a surprisingly short time.

The compass of a fibreglass sloop can often be adjusted so successfully that the residual deviation is negligible, but with some vessels this is impossible, particularly with steel and ferro-cement hulls.

The compass adjuster will leave you with a table of any deviation he has been unable to get rid of, showing what it is for each of 16 headings all round the compass. This table is called a *deviation card*.

○ The deviation on this bulkhead compass is recorded on a deviation card, which shows the error, in degrees, on each of 16 headings.

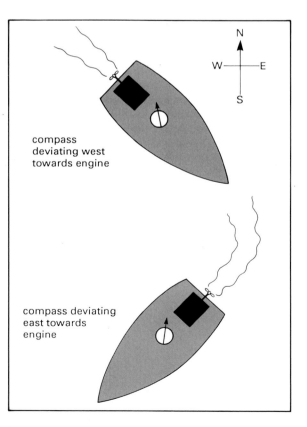

compass deviating west towards engine

compass deviating east towards engine

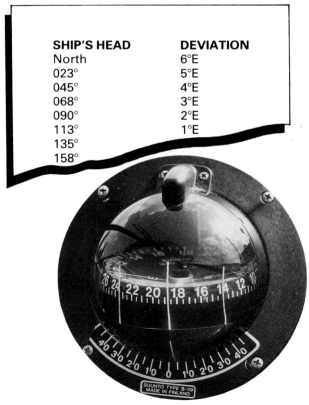

SHIP'S HEAD	DEVIATION
North	6°E
023°	5°E
045°	4°E
068°	3°E
090°	2°E
113°	1°E
135°	
158°	

The best way to present the information supplied on the deviation card is to draw a graph of the deviation, as in the illustration. This allows you to read off your deviation quickly for any ship's heading – not just the 16 selected by the compass adjuster.

When a compass is installed in a boat, great care should be taken to place it as far as reasonably possible from any fixed masses of ferrous material, such as the engine. It is up to you to stow any portable bits of metal well away from the compass to discourage it from wandering. Electrical equipment is very prone to upsetting compasses, so be particularly careful with this sort of gear. Radio speakers, for example, contain surprisingly large magnets.

Even when all these precautions have been taken there will often be some deviation.

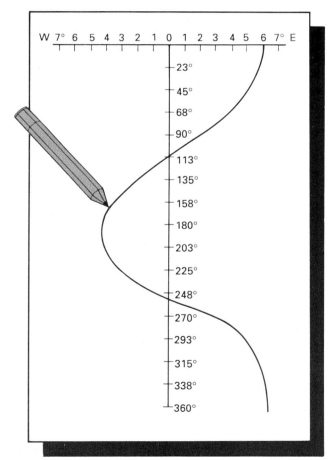

COMPASS SWINGING

If you have not employed the services of a compass adjuster, you will have to produce your own deviation card. It cannot be stressed too much that to rely on an untested compass is the height of irresponsibility. If you charter a boat, and there is no deviation card on board, you should at least run a quick check on the compass.

Running your own compass check is known as *swinging the compass*. There are various methods of doing this. Here are the two that are probably most realistic for a small yacht without special equipment.

The handbearing compass method
This is by far the quickest and simplest way of producing a deviation card. It can be done in half an hour on any stretch of calm water.

If your boat is free of ferrous metal near the stern you simply have your mate stand up by the backstay (stainless steel, of course), and check the headings of 16 courses corresponding to the old half-points of the compass: north, north-north-east, north-east, east-north-east, east, etc. The numerical values of these are the same as those in the illustration of a deviation card. You note down the difference between the compasses on each heading, and that is the deviation.

If you are uncertain about the neutrality of your magnetic dead spot you can 'swing' the handbearing compass in the following manner. Stand in the most likely spot – usually in the cockpit – take the bearing of any far distant object, then motor the boat onto the 16 headings. If the handbearing compass is reliable, the bearing will remain the same as the ship's heading varies. If it does not, move the handbearing compass to a different position until you find a suitable site.

The compass bearings method
This method is excellent if you have one of those happy vessels that can use the steering compass to take bearings. If the compass is suitably situated it is possible to sight across it and use it just like a handbearing compass. Some compasses are supplied with a clip-on 'sight' for this purpose.

◊ **A deviation curve is easy to use, and allows you to read off the deviation for any given bearing. Here the deviation at 164°M is 4°W.**

First, you need to select a suitable location for your needs. It should have calm water, a convenient charted buoy or fixed object, plenty of water and, in clear view, a conspicuous distant object which you can use to take bearings.

The method relies on the fact that if the conspicuous object is far enough away (at least five miles), then a difference in your position of a hundred yards or so won't make a significant difference to its bearing from where you are.

Having arrived at the spot, with pencil, paper and bearing sight at the ready, you now proceed to motor on each of the 16 headings previously described, while staying as close as possible to your buoy. On each heading you take the bearing of the distant object and, when you have done them all, you compare each one with the *real* magnetic bearing of the object from the buoy (which, of course, you will take from the chart). The various differences are the deviation on the 16 headings.

▷ **Motoring past a buoy on 16 headings and taking a bearing of a distant object using the steering compass will provide an accurate record of its deviation. Here the engine block is dragging the compass needle away from magnetic north.**

COMPASS SITING

Ideally the compass should be sited on the boat's centreline, in such a position that the helmsman can see it easily. It is best placed on the line between eye level and the horizon, for this will make everyone on board a better helmsman. A flick of the eye will be enough to transfer your gaze from the compass to where you are going and back again, or vice versa. There is a natural tendency to become mesmerised by peering into the compass bowl, particularly at night; if the compass is mounted in the right place it will help you stay alert.

However, it is no good having a 'perfectly' placed compass which trips up each crew member as he or she mounts the companionway to join in the action. In the end, some revolutionary from the foredeck will pacify it with a winch handle, and then you'll be sorry.

Stick it somewhere sensible, and it will guide you discreetly for a lifetime if you should choose to ask it.

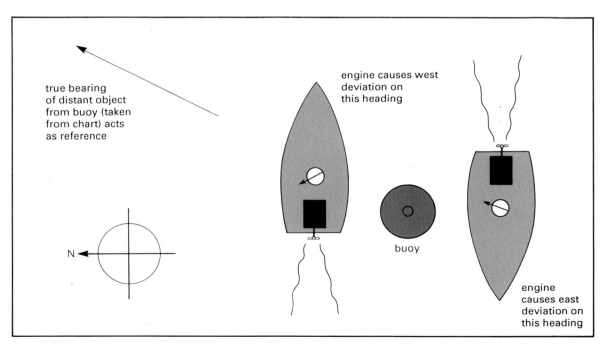

true bearing of distant object from buoy (taken from chart) acts as reference

N

engine causes west deviation on this heading

buoy

engine causes east deviation on this heading

APPLYING DEVIATION

The diagrams, and mnemonics earlier in this chapter showed how to apply variation to a true heading or a magnetic heading in order to correct one to the other.

If you now consider that the same rules apply to all compass errors, then you will experience no difficulty in dealing with deviation. For example, here is a magnetic heading:

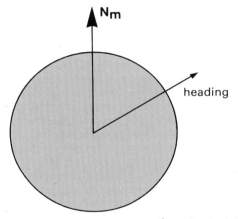

Here is the same compass heading where the deviation is to the *west*. You will see that the angle between the course and the *compass* north is *greater* than that between the course and *magnetic* north. In other words: ERROR WEST, COMPASS BEST (biggest). You must *add* the deviation to obtain a compass course.

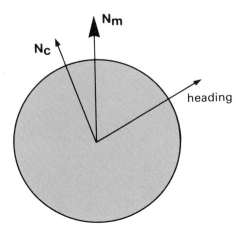

Here is the same compass heading on a different boat that has *east* deviation on this heading.

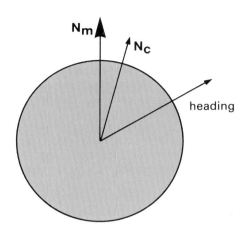

The angle between compass north and the course is *smaller* than that between magnetic north and the course, so: ERROR EAST, COMPASS LEAST. You must *subtract* the deviation to get a compass course.

Remember that deviation was measured *for a given ship's heading* and not a magnetic course. If the deviation is particularly large this should be borne in mind if you are converting from a magnetic course to a compass course.

Remember also that deviation is the relationship between the compass course and the magnetic course (or bearing), just as variation is the relationship between the magnetic and the true. So:

To convert Compass to Magnetic, apply Deviation.
To convert Magnetic to True, apply Variation.

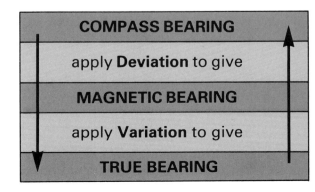

The system is generally remembered as follows:

Compass	:	**C**adbury's
apply **D**eviation	:	**D**airy
gives **M**agnetic	:	**M**ilk
apply **V**ariation	:	**V**ery
gives **T**rue	:	**T**asty

The other way up gives every sailor's favourite:

True	:	**T**imid
apply **V**ariation	:	**V**irgins
gives **M**agnetic	:	**M**ake
apply **D**eviation	:	**D**ull
gives **C**ompass	:	**C**ompanions

Example You are entering a harbour on a leading line given on the chart as 105 degrees (True from seaward). Variation is seven degrees west. Deviation on this heading is four degrees east. What is the compass course to steer?

Work up the magnetic heading first, then the compass heading:

$$
\begin{array}{rl}
& 105° \text{ T} \\
+ & \ \ 7° \quad \text{Variation west, compass best} \\
\hline
= & 112°\text{M} \\
- & \ \ 4° \quad \text{Deviation east, compass least} \\
\hline
& 108°\text{C}
\end{array}
$$

Notice that the compass heading is denoted as °C, so there is no mistake.

HEELING ERROR

All the measurements on your deviation card will have been taken when the boat was more or less upright, but the deviation of the compass may be different when the boat is heeled well over. In the nature of things it is almost impossible to calibrate this. If you get settled on a course with the boat heeled, the best thing you can do is to check your heading with the handbearing compass.

It is a good thing to do this anyway, because deviation can change from month to month, and it takes very little effort to be reasonably sure where you stand.

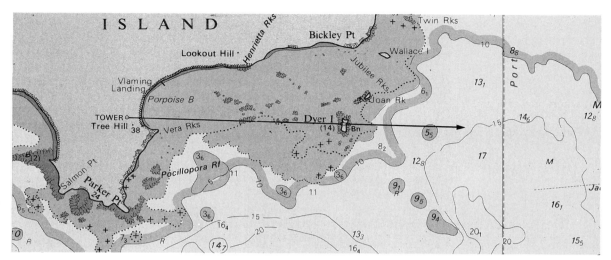

COMPASS NOTES

A first-class way to check your compass is to note your compass heading when you are steering straight up a transit that is definable on your chart. If there are enough transits around it is possible to produce a complete compass swing by doing this, and the card so produced would be accurate indeed.

You can keep a note of any discrepancy and be particularly careful on that heading the next time.

☞ A glance at your steering compass as you sail up a well-defined transit will show up any deviation – but remember to allow for variation before you suspect the compass itself.

If you are heeled hard as you run up a transit, you have a perfect opportunity to check your heeling error for that heading. Note it down, and label it *port* tack or *starboard* tack.

Treat your compass with great respect. No matter how much you paid for it, it is only as good as its installation and the accuracy of its deviation curve.

5 The Estimated Position

Navigation consists of two main arts. The first is knowing where you are, and the second is deciding how to get from there to where you want to go.

When you want to know your whereabouts while on passage, you must make an estimate of your position. You can then go on to check this in various ways.

The ship's log

Before you can begin to work out where you are now, you need to know where you have been. To be able to make back-reference to known positions and events you must keep a *log book* to record them all. This need not be an expensively-bound volume; a stiff-backed exercise book of the type available in most stationers is quite sufficient. You can rule in your own columns: Time, Log, Course, Weather and Event are sufficient headings for most people, though some like to add Estimated Leeway.

THE DEAD RECKONING POSITION (DR)

This is a position worked up using only the simple elements of distance run and course steered.

Distance run is easy enough to work out. It is simply a matter of reading your log to see how far you have come through the water from your last known (or estimated) position. So long as your log is accurate, then that is that.

Course steered is a little more interesting, but essentially quite simple. It is the course taken from the steering compass, corrected for variation, deviation and, if necessary, leeway.

▷ **A typical entry in the ship's log book should look something like this.**

LEEWAY

It is in the nature of things that a sailing vessel when close-hauled will be going sideways as well as forwards. This is known as leeway. As she turns progressively further from the wind her leeway will decrease until, on a dead run, she is making none at all. The same applies to vessels under power though, if they are deep-draughted, to a lesser extent.

How much leeway you are making varies enormously with the boat and the conditions. A large deep-keeled modern cruising sloop close-hauled on a fine day in calm water may be making less than five degrees, and virtually nothing on a beam reach. The same vessel thrashing to windward offshore in a whole gale could well be making 10 or 12 degrees of leeway, while a 28-foot bilge-keeler in the same conditions could be making as much as 20 degrees.

▷ **Leeway can make a big difference to your progress. Here the helmsman is steering 045°T, but the actual 'wake course' of the boat is 052°T. In other words, the boat is making seven degrees of leeway.**

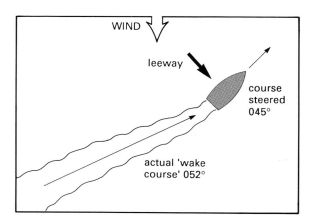

TIME	LOG	COURSE	WEATHER	EVENT
1530	27.8	135°M	SW3 FAIR 1014✓	OWERS LIGHT CLOSE TO PORT

Plotting with leeway

When you are estimating your position the best way to handle leeway on the chart is to correct your 'course steered' line before you plot it. Set your plotter for the course steered, put it on the chart, and then imagine it blown *downwind* seven degrees, or however many degrees it is. Then draw the line. In theory this is navigational heresy, but if you draw a 'course steered'

and then a 'wake course' as well, you will end up with a confusion of lines on the chart.

Estimating leeway

There are various ways of estimating leeway, all of them more or less guesswork. The simplest way is to align yourself with the fore-and-aft line of the boat, and look at the angle of your wake. This can be seen

CHECKING THE LOG

An accurate log is vital to your navigation. To check it, take the opportunity to motor at a steady speed in both directions along a measured mile (there are a number of these around the coasts of Britain). You should do this as near as possible to slack water. Check the time you took to do each run, add the times together, divide by two and then compare the result with the time given to cover one mile at your speed in the 'Measured Mile' tables in your almanac. Express any difference as a percentage inaccuracy in your instrument and note it down.

If you can, you should do this once or twice a season, and build up a long-term pattern of results which will increase your confidence and your accuracy.

↪ **Measured miles are to be found throughout the world. Each is marked by a conspicuous transit at either end, and you must motor at 90 degrees to the transit lines to achieve an accurate result.**

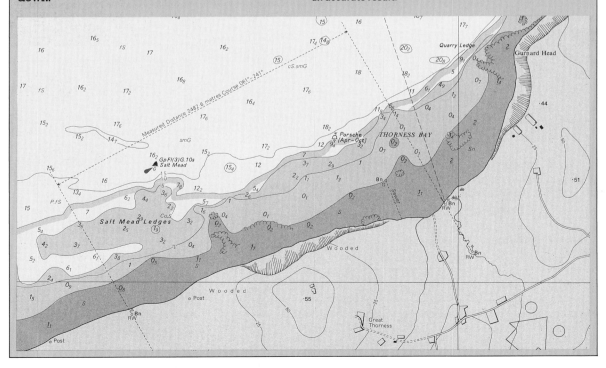

more clearly if you are using a log with a long line, since it is easier to estimate the angle of the log line. Try using a big Douglas Protractror held close to the eye to 'guestimate' the angle.

Another way to assess your leeway is to throw a heavy floating object over the stern and check its position relative to your fore-and-aft line after a short while. The helmsman should steer as straight as possible, and you should throw in a really solid item. A log of wood is the best thing, or even the body of a mutineer if you can catch one. It is no good using something which the wind can blow sideways.

In practice, a dead reckoning position is produced by plotting the course steered (corrected for leeway) and the distance run along that course. It is marked on the chart by the symbol +. On its own, a DR position isn't a lot of use in tidal waters, but it is the basis from which you work up an *estimated position*.

◊ If your boat is equipped with a long log line, its angle to the fore-and-aft line of the boat indicates the leeway. Try to assess it by lining up a Douglas Protractor with the transom or pushpit rail.

◇ To apply leeway on the chart, simply move the plotter in the appropriate direction. Here the course steered is 055°T (below), but the boat is making seven degrees of leeway. The plotter is rotated seven degrees downwind to give a 'course made good' of 062°T (below right).

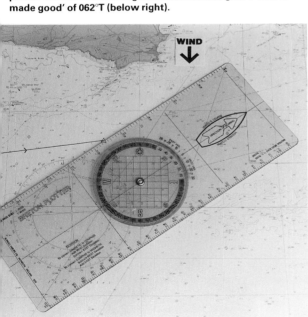

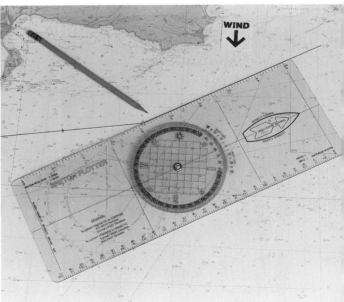

THE ESTIMATED POSITION (EP)

An estimated position, or EP, is a dead reckoning position corrected for leeway and for the tidal stream.

When you are plotting an EP, the first thing to do is check your log book for the last known estimated position and, starting from there, plot the current DR on the chart, correcting for leeway as usual.

You then look up the tidal stream information, using either the tidal atlas or the tidal diamonds on the chart, and plot a *tidal vector* beginning at your DR position.

If you are using tidal diamonds, the chart information will give you an exact direction for this. Like all directions and bearings printed on the chart, it will be in degrees True.

The information in the atlas is of a more pictorial nature, but it is surprising how accurately you can transfer the direction of a tide arrow from the atlas onto your chart. If you are plotting an EP for one hour's distance run, then the number of miles length of the tidal vector will be the number of knots of given tidal stream. If the vector is for more than one hour, or less, you will need to adjust its length accordingly.

▷ To plot an EP, you start with your current DR, worked up from your last EP or fix using the log book information and correcting for leeway (left). You then draw a tidal vector from the DR, using the best tidal information to hand. Here a convenient tidal diamond provides a direction and rate for the tidal stream.

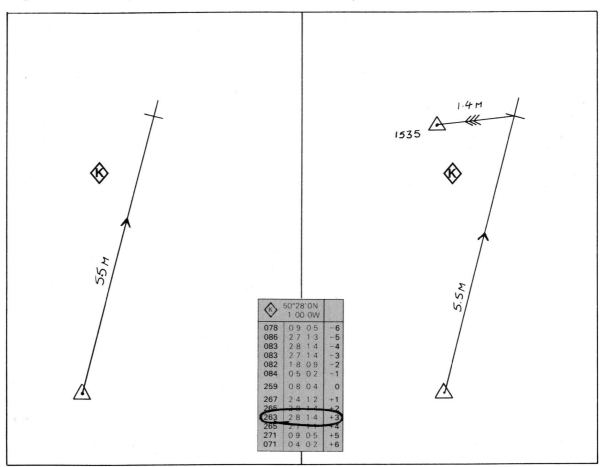

TIME	LOG	COURSE	WEATHER	EVENT
1535	71.5	020° M	SSE6 Rain	EP on chart

⇦ Enter your EP in the log like this.

To sum up:

1 Plot your DR, corrected if necessary for leeway, from your last known or estimated position. Note that a course line always has the symbol of one arrow in the middle.

2 Check your tidal information.

3 Plot the tidal vector from the DR position, and mark your estimated position as shown. An EP is always shown as a triangle with a time. A tidal vector is always given the three arrow symbol.

4 Enter the EP in the log book.

When to plot an EP

When you are on a passage you should either know where you are at all times, or be able to work it out in a very short time indeed. If you update your position hourly you will be able to do this.

On a long offshore passage you may feel that an hourly update is unnecessary, and there are times when this is undoubtedly true. Experience will tell you in the end, but if you are in doubt, then one position every hour is a useful guide.

If it is more than an hour since your last EP you will need to work out your tide vector for more than one hour of tide on a 'pro-rata' basis. Even if you are

exactly on time the hours in your log book may not coincide with the hours of the tide, in which case you must make the necessary adjustments. To make life easier you can often arrange to plot your EPs just on the 'tidal hour' as you turn the next page in the atlas. This saves a lot of needless tedium.

Sometimes, particularly if you are beating to windward, you will change course frequently between EPs. In such circumstances you will probably feel disinclined to spend much time down below. If this is so, do not try to work up a separate EP for every course change, for that is the road to madness. Simply log each course change as it happens and, when you are ready, plot all the DRs and then plot the tide vectors, in whole hours, onto the final DR. Here is an example:

TIME	LOG	COURSE	WEATHER	EVENT
0600	13.6	135°M	E4 1018	Close-hauled on port. Owers lightship close to port.
0633	15.8	035°M	E4 1018	Tacked.
0715	19.1	120°M	E4 1018	Tacked onto port.
0900	27.2	030°M	E5 1020	EP on chart. Close-hauled on starboard

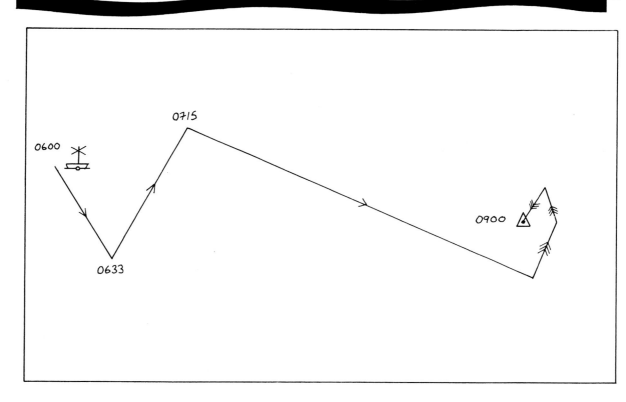

Checking your EP

Don't expect too much from an estimated position. Its very name gives it away. It may surprise you with its accuracy, or it may lead to tooth-grinding despair. The thing to do is to *check it if you can*, with a fix if possible.

At worst, you can switch on your echo sounder (as soon as you read the log, not five minutes later!) Then reduce the depth to soundings (see Chapter 2), and see if it confirms or rejects your EP. If it appears to confirm it then, depending on how varied the bottom configuration is, you can have a little more confidence in your position. If it rejects it, then you should look around and think carefully about what may have gone wrong.

A final word of warning. As with all navigation, it does not do to forget that you are not sailing a chart table around the sea, and that if your EP turns out to be in error, the rocks and shoals are very hard indeed. If in doubt, *assume the worst*.

6 Position Fixing

In chapter four we decided that having worked up an estimated position (EP), the next thing to do was to check it and see whether or not it made sense. You must do this by *fixing your position*. Although the fix is a defined position, it isn't necessarily closely defined, and evaluating the quality of a fix is an important part of your job.

Fixes may be obtained by traditional or electronic means. Since an electronic fix is not always available (and may require further checking even if it is), we shall first consider the classical methods.

CHARTED OBJECTS

After plotting an EP you should check around to see if you are close to a charted object, such as a buoy. What is meant by 'close' will depend on how accurate you need to be, but if you are well offshore, and within a cable (200 yards) or two of an object, then you can consider your position fixed. For example, '1½ cables to the southward of DZ3 buoy'.

POSITION LINES

If there is no handy marker you will need to use position lines (PLs) derived from charted objects that are further away. These should be selected so as to give the best possible 'cut'.

If you take the case of two position lines crossing at 90 degrees you can see that a three-degree error in the bearing on one line will not throw the fix too far out. If the position lines converge at 10 degrees, the results of the same error are catastrophic.

▽ The effect of a three-degree bearing error when the 'cut' is poor (A) and good (B). The navigator at B can be much more confident of his position.

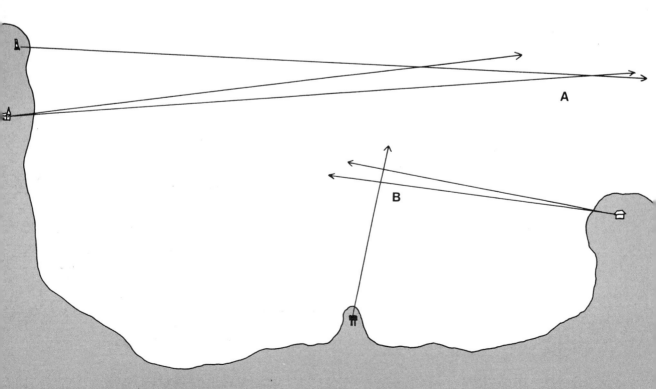

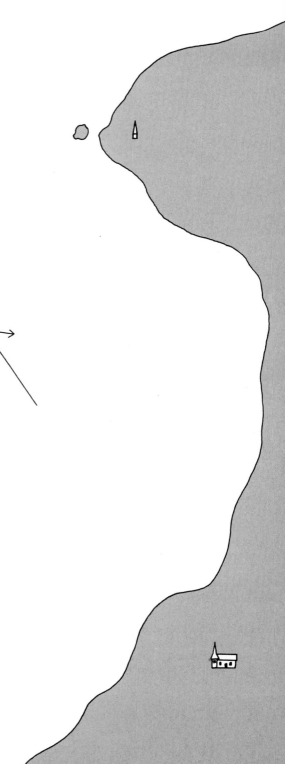

The effects of such errors are made worse if you take bearings on very distant objects. A three-degree bearing error on a nearby buoy will make little difference when you come to plot it on the chart, but a three-degree bearing error on a lighthouse six miles away will result in a plot that is over a quarter of a mile out. So if you have any choice, you should always try to fix your position using closer objects.

When three or more decent position lines are available you should try to select the ones that will give a 'cocked hat' that looks like this:

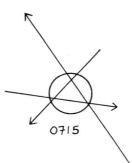

0715

Note that it has a circle round it to denote a fix, and the time at which is was taken. Note also that the PLs are short, neat lines. There is no need to draw the line all the way from the object when you are plotting your fix.

If your bearings are such that the cocked hat is nice and tight, so much the better, but if your fix is enormous, then the best you have achieved is an 'area of position'. Treat it with care and assume the worst. Better still, try a fourth position line to see if you can narrow things down – or scrap it and start again.

SOURCES OF POSITION LINES

Source: Transit set up ashore for the assistance of navigators (e.g. harbour leading marks). These may be lights or daymarks.

Likely quality: Excellent.

↻ **Here leading beacons show a safe passage through rocks.**

Source: Two fixed objects in line, forming a natural transit.

Likely quality: Excellent.

↻ **This transit of the pier head with the church spire gives an excellent position line on the chart (right).**

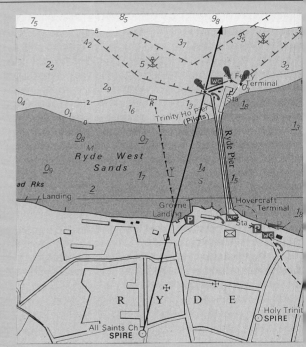

Source: A fixed object and a buoy.

Likely quality: Very good, but not perfect since buoys may drift a short distance off station.

↻ **Here a church spire is aligned with a buoy to provide a very useful transit.**

Source: Two headlands in line, or a headland and a beacon.

Likely quality: Very good, but you may have some difficulty deciding where a headland 'bites the sea' in an area of big tides.

◊ **Here a headland is aligned with a beacon.**

A transit of any kind is nearly always to be preferred over a compass bearing because it is not subject to the inevitable small compass errors experienced in yachts. However, you must check each transit with a compass bearing. This will both make sure you have the right one, and provide a ready check on the accuracy of your compass.

Source: Sectors of lights (see Chapter 9).

Likely quality: Very good, depending how sharp the cut-off is.

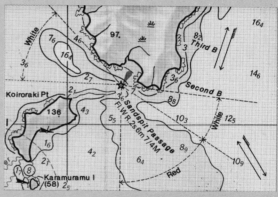

Source: Auxiliary lights on lighthouses (see Chapter 9).

Likely quality: Similar to above.

◄ **Coloured light sectors provide excellent position lines at night.**

Source: Compass bearing of fixed object ashore.

Likely quality: Good, depending on distance and conditions.

◊ **If you are reduced to taking a bearing, choose a really conspicuous fixed object, close to.**

SOURCES OF POSITION LINES (CONTINUED)

Source: Bearing of a buoy.

Likely quality: Good, depending on distance and conditions, but be aware that the buoy may be slightly off station.

◊ **The more important the buoy, the more accurate its position is likely to be.**

Source: Bearing of the side of an island or headland, expressed as LHS or RHS (left or right hand side).

Likely quality: Fair, owing to problems deciding where the shore 'bites the sea'.

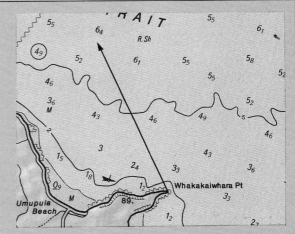

◊ **A headland must be well defined to be any use as a source of position lines.**

Source: Radio lighthouse (see Chapter 7).

Likely quality: Excellent, if there is one!

Source: Compass bearings of RDF stations (see Chapter 7).

Likely quality: Variable between good and poor.

◊ **This major lighthouse doubles as an RDF station.**

POSITION FIXING BY ECHO SOUNDER

When you are using the echo sounder as a source of position lines, or to check a fix or estimated position, all depths must be reduced to soundings (see Chapter 2). How accurately you do this will depend on the circumstances; common sense will decide on the day.

The line of soundings

In poor visibility, or fog (visibility of a thousand metres or less) you will often be reduced to log, compass and echo sounder to deduce your position.

One way you can do this, especially if the bottom is uneven, is to take a series of soundings as you steer a straight course, and log each one carefully. if you then plot these on a piece of the hard toilet paper recommended by most manufacturers of marine plumbing, and offer it up to the chart like tracing paper, you may be able to discover your whereabouts by finding a section of the seabed with which it appears to coincide.

The course line (corrected, if necessary, for tide and leeway) has now become the position line on which you were situated at the time of the last sounding.

Running a contour

If you are trying to make port in fog, one sure way to success is to steer a course from your last known position to a point on the shore which is definitely to one side or the other of your destination. While you are running in, you work out the depth of water at the sea buoy, entry beacon or pier head, and when you reach water of that depth you turn towards the harbour.

You can run along the depth contour by turning 15 degrees in towards the shore until the water shoals, and then 40 degrees out again until it becomes deeper. Then turn back in towards the shore again. Keep doing this, and you will be sailing along a very convoluted, but perfectly valid position line towards your destination. In due course it will loom up out of the fog.

You must take care to select suitable harbours and suitable contours for this technique, but there are many which are fine for the job. What you need is an approach free of dangers, and a good, positive contour line with no awkward bends or underwater 'bays' in it.

▷ **If you hope to zigzag down a contour in the fog, choose a contour line that takes you to an identifiable point, as directly as possible.**

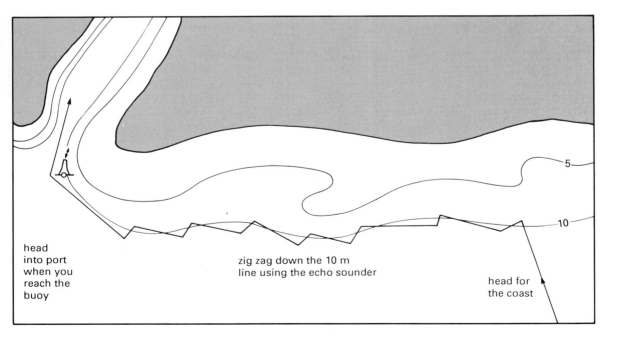

head
into port
when you
reach the
buoy

zig zag down the 10 m
line using the echo sounder

head for
the coast

Contour as a single position line

Whenever the reading on your depth sounder changes from one side to another of a depth shown on the chart as a contour, you have crossed a position line defined by the relevant contour on that chart. This can be really useful if, for example, you have a single compass bearing on a lighthouse. If the bottom is shelving in such a way as to make the contours smooth and even, reference to the depth will supply a reasonable second position line as shown in the example below.

Using depth to check a fix

Whatever the circumstances, you should always check the depth of water under a fix of any kind. A fix, after all, is only the point of coincidence of a lot of information, so an extra clue can do no possible harm. If you have made a nasty mistake, perhaps by pretending to yourself (as we all do sometimes) that what you are seeing is what you hope to see, then reference to the echo sounder as the final arbiter may well save the day.

THE CIRCULAR POSITION LINE

When you have only one object in sight, a circular position line with the object at its centre will often cross with a compass bearing to give you quite a good fix. If you know how far off you are, you can set up your dividers (or preferably a pair of compasses) to that distance and scribe the arc of a circle on the chart across the position line from the compass bearing.

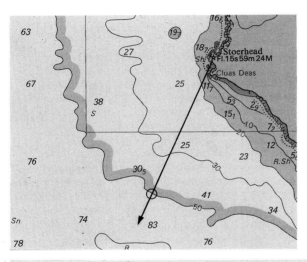

◊ **Here a bearing on a conspicuous shore object is crossed with a contour line deduced from the depth sounder to give a rough fix.**

◇ **If you know your distance from, say, a lighthouse, you can draw a circular position line. When crossed with a bearing on the light this will give you a fix.**

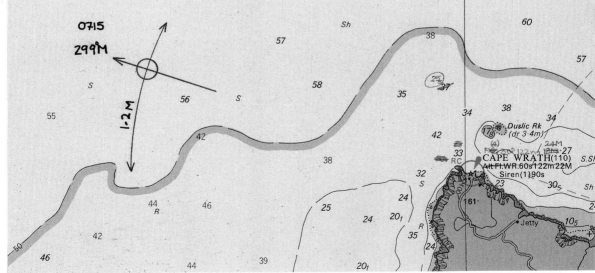

Distance off by rising and dipping lights

The simplest way of ascertaining 'distance off' is by noting the time a lighthouse rises over the horizon as you sail towards it, or dips below the horizon as you sail away.

When making a night or twilight landfall you invariably pick up one lighthouse first. It is very reassuring to put a fix on the chart as soon as the light appears by taking its bearing and then consulting the rising and dipping table in the almanac to see how far off you are.

▽ **Part of the rising and dipping table in the almanac. You simply cross the height of the light with your height of eye to obtain a distance off.**

Height of light		Height of eye		
		metres	1	2	③
metres	feet	feet	3	7	10
10	33		8.7	9.5	10.2
12	39		9.3	10.1	10.8
14	46		9.9	10.7	11.4
16	53		10.4	11.2	11.9
18	59		10.9	11.7	12.4
20	66		11.4	12.2	12.9
㉒	72		11.9	12.7	⑬.4
24	79		12.3	13.1	13.8
26	85		12.7	13.5	14.2
28	92		13.1	13.9	14.6

Distance off by vertical sextant angle

The other way of determining distance off a single object is by measuring the vertical angle between the object and the waterline. To do this you need a sextant. This will measure to an astonishing degree of accuracy the angle you are seeing.

Correcting and using a sextant are covered in detail in *Celestial Navigation,* also published by Fernhurst Books. Since you are unlikely to have a sextant unless you are learning celestial, it is assumed here that, if you have one, you are already familiar with the techniques for using it.

The most popular objects to use for the vertical sextant angle method are lighthouses, so remember that the height given on the chart is the height of the *lantern* above MHWS. Depending upon the accuracy you require you may or may not decide to correct this figure for the current height of tide.

Having measured the angle, taken a bearing of the object, and noted the log reading (and the depth), you then enter the table in the almanac headed 'Distance off by vertical sextant angle' and read off your range, which is given in miles and cables.

▽ **If you have a sextant, you can use it to establish the altitude of a charted object such as a lighthouse lantern. Relating this to the appropriate table in the almanac will give you a distance off.**

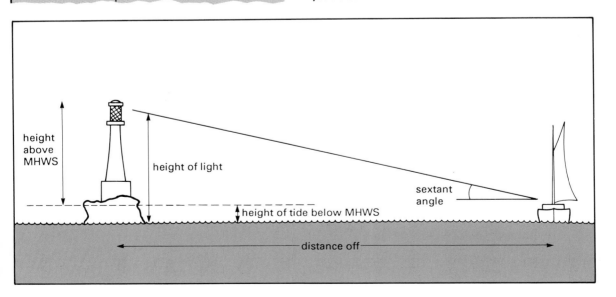

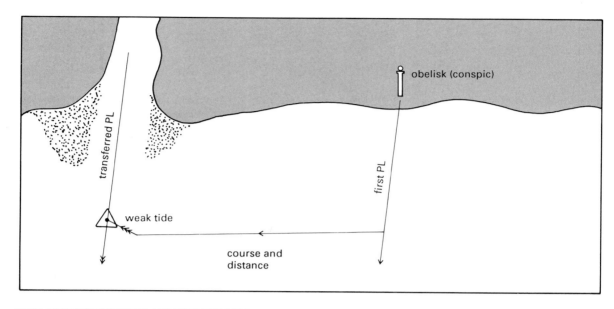

labels on figure: obelisk (conspic), transferred PL, first PL, weak tide, course and distance

THE TRANSFERRED POSITION LINE

If you need a position line and there is absolutely nothing available to give you one, you can produce one out of your hat by transferring a PL, taken some time ago, up to your present estimated position.

Suppose, for example, you are running along a stretch of coastline looking for the way into a river whose entry is notoriously difficult to spot. A mile or two before you are due to reach the entry you sight a day mark on the shore. Wait until the bearing of the day mark is that of the course required to enter the river and then note it down and log it.

You then draw another line parallel to your position line, running into the entrance of the river. This is your *transferred position line*. Note it has two arrows on the end. All you have to do is work out the distance to sail *through the water* allowing for any tide that may be running between the PL and the transferred PL. When you have 'run your distance' you turn onto your heading and run into the river mouth up your transferred position line.

Transferred position lines are generally not of very good quality because of all the possible sources of error. Courses steered may be inaccurate because of compass errors, tidal anomalies, or even poor steering. The technique should therefore be avoided unless you have no alternative.

◠ Using a transferred PL to find a river mouth (see text).

◊ For a running fix, take two bearings on the same object (top). Then work up an estimated position from PL1 (centre). Then draw a line through the EP, parallel to PL1 (bottom). The point where it cuts PL2 is the running fix.

Running fix

Sometimes you have a single object in view, and you need a fix. This often happens when passing an isolated lighthouse at night. Here is the technique:

1. Take a bearing on the lighthouse and log it (PL1).
2. Run as far as you need to take another bearing which would make a reasonable 'cut' with the first if they were intersecting. Log this as well (PL2).
3. Choose any point on PL1, and use it to work up an estimated position for the time and distance run between the taking of the two bearings.
4. Transfer PL1 so that it runs through the EP. Where the transferred PL1 cuts PL2, that is your *running fix*. Log it, check it for depth and evaluate it.

Occasionally you need a fix on a single object but you have no time to run the distance needed to produce a classic running fix. If that is the case, do you have one or more position lines in a previous fix that you can run up to this one? If you do, give it a try and check it with depth. It's not much, but it may be all you have.

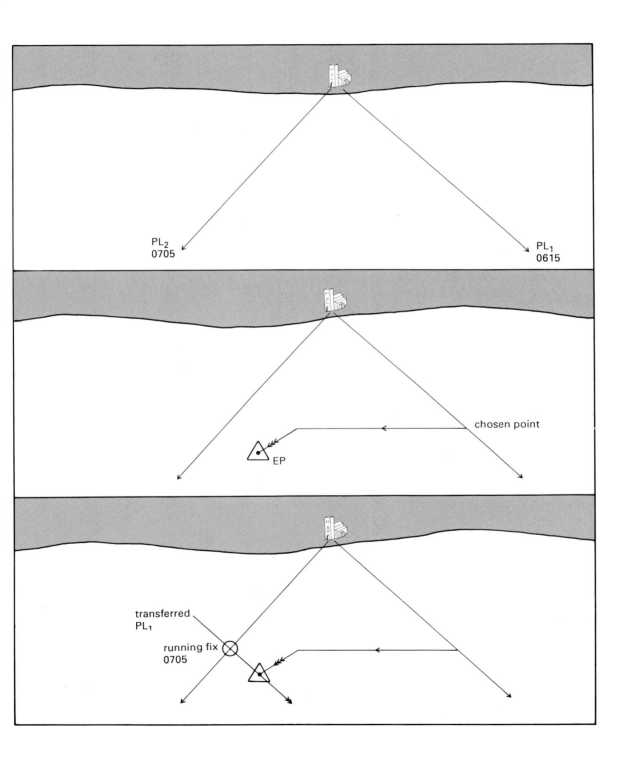

PL$_2$
0705

PL$_1$
0615

chosen point

EP

transferred
PL$_1$

running fix
0705

ABEAM AND FOUR-POINT BEARING

There are all sorts of 'rules of thumb' for determining your approximate distance off an object. There is no room to discuss them all here, but one technique is well worth a mention. The distance off it gives may not be brilliantly accurate in practice but if you are alone on watch at night as you sail by a single lighthouse or buoy, you might be glad of a system that is a lot less trouble than a running fix.

This is what you do. When the object bears four points (45 degrees) relative to your ship's head, note the log reading. When the object is abeam (90 degrees to the ship's head) note the log again and make any adjustments necessary to correct it for tidal stream, since what you are looking for is your distance run over the ground. This distance is the same as your distance off.

When you are sailing along the coast, the tide is usually more or less directly with you or against you, so it is a straight addition or subtraction to convert your logged distance run into distance run over the ground. Clearly the system won't work if you have reason to suspect a strong cross-set.

▷ **The abeam and four-point bearing is a useful technique to have up your sleeve. Note the log reading when an object bears 45 degrees from the ship's head, and note the reading again when it is directly abeam. In theory, the distance run over the ground is the same as your distance off.**

LOGGING FIXES

A fix tells you where you were at a given time. Your boat is moving on through the water so you should take the bearings as quickly as possible, and then immediately note the *time* and the *log reading*. You should also check the depth as a matter of course to see if it agrees with your fix.

If you don't log your fix accurately you may as well not have bothered to take it.

DEFINITION OF POSITION

The positions of objects at sea are often given in terms of their latitude and longitude. Plotting such positions should cause no problems.

You rarely need to define your own position in these absolute terms, but occasionally you may need to let others know where you are – particularly if you are unfortunate enough to be on the radio in distress.

Most people find it tiresome, and a potential source of wild inaccuracy, to try to plot their latitude and longitude position in a hurry. A safer method is to note where you are with reference to some obvious feature of the coast. For example: 'My position is 070 degrees from St Helen's Fort, 1.2 miles'.

It is understood by one and all that all bearings thus given are in degrees *True*.

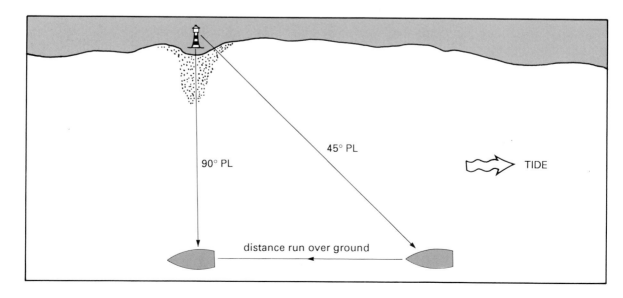

90° PL   45° PL   TIDE

distance run over ground

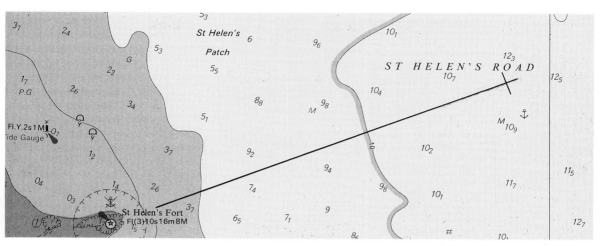

⌂ In communications, always try to define your position with reference to some coastal feature. Note that the bearing is always given FROM the coastal feature.

TRANSFERRING POSITIONS

From time to time it is necessary to transfer a fix or estimated position from one chart to the next. More than one staunch vessel has been wrecked because of errors in doing this.

Be *very* careful when transferring latitude and longitude positions. Remember that longitude numbers increase west of Greenwich from *right to left*. When you are east of Greenwich, they increase from *left to right*.

Another way is to transfer the position by relating it to a salient feature that is on both charts. Then the only mistake you can make is omitting to reset the dividers if the scales of the charts are different. DON'T DO IT. GET IT RIGHT!

If you make a rule always to transfer by both methods, then you really cannot go wrong.

7 Electronic Aids to Navigation

In recent years there has been a tremendous upsurge in the availability and usefulness of radio aids to navigation. These can now be said to fall into two main categories.

- Those which supply a source for single position lines.
- Position fixing systems, either of the hyperbolic type (Decca and Loran) or those using navigational satellites.

Although the former are rapidly being rendered obsolete by the latter, the old-fashioned systems can still be of considerable use, so they will be considered later in the chapter.

The essence of good position-finding is to throw as much information as possible into the melting-pot. As we have seen, the quality of each piece of data must be assessed so that if there appears to be a discrepancy you can make a safe, sensible decision. The one certain thing is that to base any important decision upon only one of a variety of possible sources of input is the height of folly.

The advent of modern electronic fixing aids has not changed this. The Decca, Loran and satellite navigation systems are wonderful things. They are capable of producing a fixes of remarkable accuracy out of thin air in conditions when the navigator using classical methods is left with his echo-sounder, his magnetic compass, his log, and his look-out. All of these latter are subject to inbuilt errors. The electronically obtained position can be extremely accurate, BUT IT IS STILL ONLY A FIX and, like all fixes, it exists merely to verify and purify our estimated position.

So long as they are seen in this light, electronic fixing systems are of immense vale to the competent navigator. It should never be forgotten, however, that since the dawn of time people have managed without them and that it is perfectly possible to do so still.

DECCA

Decca (and/or Loran C) is currently (1990) the most useful electronic aid available to the North Atlantic coastal navigator.

A Decca Navigator will produce a fix at any time so that the system offers a constant up-date on the yacht's position. Often the degree of accuracy obtained is remarkable, though from time to time it is no better than a cocked hat worked up from three magnetic bearings observed from a heaving deck. The dark side of this sort of instant pinpoint fixing is that one comes to rely upon it implicitly, so that on the rare occasions when results are far worse than expected, the unwise navigator can find himself in real trouble.

Decca is subject to two kinds of error: *fixed* and *variable*. **Fixed errors** are inherent in the signal system which the on-board receiver is processing. Some areas of the coast are free of them entirely, while others, such as parts of the Bristol Channel, are particularly prone to their effects. It is possible to obtain information indicating where fixed errors are to be found, and what their magnitude will be, but to use this properly you have to equip the yacht with 'Decca' charts and then plot your fix from the Decca coordinates themselves rather than a Lat/Long read-out or a distance and bearing to a *way-point,* which is by far the most sensible method to use on small vessels.

If you do not care to go into such detail in your search for accuracy, a 'one-off' glance at a fixed error sheet for your area will indicate the zones where the errors are situated. Once this is established, you know that in those waters you must not expect too much from your Decca.

Whether or not a set is suffering from the presence of a fixed error, all Decca receivers are subject to periodic **variable errors.** These are produced by phenomena such as sunset and sunrise, thunderstorms and sunspot activity. They can produce results varying from a minor inaccuracy to a total wipeout.

From the above warnings, the basic message must now be clear. DO NOT RELY IMPLICITLY UPON YOUR DECCA, just as you would not rely on any other single source of navigational input to the exclusion of all others.

So long as the system is seen merely as another source of information for the navigator's pudding mix, the potential for errors need not be a matter for undue concern. When navigating using Decca as the

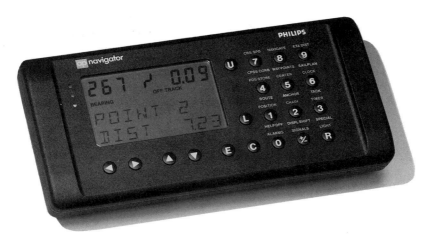

main fixing method, it is vital that a conventional plot is kept running. If an anomaly appears in the Decca plot, it will show up as a discrepancy against the EP, or against any other fixing technique that may be in use at the time.

As soon as a question mark begins to hover spectrally over a Decca plot, other position lines must immediately be sought. Failing all else, a simple echo-sounding may resolve the question. No experienced skipper expects wonders from an EP, and in the majority of cases the Decca will be proved right, but *it must be checked*. If there were no Decca, and a serious argument arose between an apparently tight cocked hat and a carefully worked up EP, the navigator would not rest until he had found the source of the discrepancy. What, then, is so different if the fix has been produced by the Decca?

The answer is, of course, noothing at all.

Decca can provide a good navigator with a quantum leap forward in accuracy, and it can save him a great deal of work, but for the foolish man who is deluded into the belief that he can purchase skill and experience in a high-impact plastic box, it may prove to be the most lethal 'safety aid' on the market.

SATELLITE NAVIGATION SYSTEMS

For some years now **Satnav** receivers have been readily available. These operate on the signals of a number of orbiting 'transit' satellites, and the fixes they offer are extremely useful for ocean-going yachts. Unfortunately, for the coastal and offshore

◁ **This Decca-type navigator is showing the bearing and distance to a previously-defined waypoint, and is also indicating that the ship is 0.09 miles off-track to starboard.**

navigator operating in tidal waters, they suffer from one great problem. They can only deliver a fix when the satellites are suitably placed. Often these times may be an hour or more apart.

In between fixes the machine will, if 'interfaced' with log and compass, work up a DR, but this is of little use to the mariner sailing in tide-swept coastal waters. He would do far better investing in a Decca, or waiting another year or two until the new and astonishingly accurate GPS Navstar (Global Positioning System) satellite arrangement becomes affordable.

GPS Navstar operates on an entirely different system from the 'transit' satellite navigator and appears to come as near to providing all the answers as we are likely to get. Fixes can be enjoyed 24 a hours a day with an accuracy of up to 100 metres (the system is capable of 10-metre accuracy, but the US military who operate it will not release this to the public). It suffers from no unforeseen errors. By 1991 it seems likely that sets will be on sale at a price comparable with a good Decca receiver.

For the navigator who wants confirmation of whether he's on the bow or the stern of his yacht, GPS Navstar seems to be first-class investment, but just as with Decca, a short, damp future awaits the user who doesn't run an old-fashioned plot just in case someone shoots down the satellites, or pulls out the plug in the master station.

CALAIS MAIN LT 50°57'.7N 1°51'.3E	Count of beats	Bearing of Lt Ho from seaward (degrees)									
		0	1	2	3	4	5	⑥	7	8	9
Morse ident: **CL** — · — · · — · ·	0	—	—	·	—	—	—	—	090	092	094
Frequency: Ch 88 (162.025 MHz)	10	096	098	100	102	104	106	108	110	112	114
Range: 20 n miles	20	116	118	120	122	124	126	128	130	132	134
Times: H24 (transmits	㉚	136	138	140	142	144	146	⑭⑧	150	152	154
alternately with	40	156	158	160	162	164	166	168	170	172	174
North Foreland Lt)	50	176	178	180	182	184	186	188	190	192	194
	60	196	198	200	202	204	206	208	210	—	—

THE RADIO LIGHTHOUSE

There are several of these transmitting stations around the UK coast, but as they are being operated on an experimental basis there is no guarantee, at the time of writing, that they will be with us long.

If you have a VHF radio able to receive channel 88 you need no further special equipment to use these aids. The signal consists simply of a morse identification followed by a series of beats or pulses. You count the pulses and refer to a table in your almanac; this gives you the bearing of the lighthouses in degrees True to a most acceptable level of accuracy.

RADIO DIRECTION FINDING

Radio Direction Finding (RDF) is all but obsolete in the 1990s. It is far less accurate than the other electronic aids, it is comparatively cumbersome to use and it requires considerable skill on the part of the operator. However, it is with us yet, and for some sailors it is still the only extra help they can call upon in poor visibility. It can also provide a useful back-up for the more sophisticated modern system.

RDF works like this: a series of specially established non-directional transmitting stations send out signals, either continuously or periodically. The signals consist of a simple morse identification code followed by a continuous tone. You tune your RDF receiver to a station and, by means of the receiver's directional ferrite rod aerial, ascertain the direction of the signal. When the aerial is lined up with the station the signal will be at its *weakest*. This is called a *null*. Since most modern RDF sets have a compass attached to the aerial you can then take the bearing of the null just as if it were a buoy.

△ The almanac information for a radio lighthouse. In this case 36 pulses indicate a bearing of 148°T.

RDF TRANSMITTERS

RDF transmitters are placed at strategic points around the coasts of most countries in the developed world. Every effort has been made to site them where they will be most useful as single sources of position lines (as on harbour breakwaters), and where they will provide the best cuts and cocked hats for two-point and three-point fixes.

Their ranges vary a lot. Some of the small ones, such as Chichester Bar, have a range of only ten miles or so, while the mighty radio beacons of Barra Head and Round Island reach out up to 200 miles into the Atlantic. They are indicated on the chart by the symbol ⊙ RC, but this merely gives notice of their presence. For details of their use and specification you should refer to your almanac, or to the Admiralty List of Radio Signals.

▽ Chichester Bar radio beacon, a small RDF transmitter on the south coast of England.

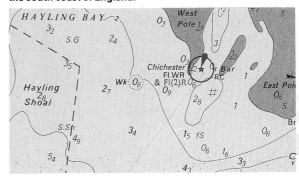

No	Name	Lat/Long	Ident		Freq	Mode	Range	Notes
33	Nab Tower Lt	50°40'.0N 00°57'.1W	NB	— · — · · ·	312.6	A2A	10nm	

A number of RDF beacons have been established for the use of aircraft, and these are very useful to the marine navigator. These aerobeacons use the same chart symbol as the marine beacons, except that the circle has the legend Aero RC beside it. Details of their signals are also listed in the almanacs. Often, an aerobeacon is not shown on a chart. If this is the case, extract its latitude and longitude from your almanac, and plot its position.

Because there are a lot of beacons using a comparatively small range of frequencies, and also for the convenience of the navigator, certain beacons are arranged together in groups. All the beacons in a group operate on the same frequency but at different times, so you can listen to one after another without having to retune your set. Each beacon operates for a period of one minute and is followed immediately by the next beacon in the group. When the last beacon has given out its signal, the first one begins again.

The grouped beacons are numbered sequentially and the almanacs contain a table giving the times that each number in the sequence starts up. Because it is rare to be able to hear all the beacons in a given group from one location there are often periods of silence in the sequence, so it is helpful to know when to listen out for the one you want.

▷ A group of beacons, with a chart showing the transmission times of each beacon in the sequence.

Beacons that are not grouped with any others are continuous, so they can be heard all the time you are within range. Most aerobeacons are continuous, and this is one of their useful features.

The tabulated information for all these beacons is shown in the almanacs. An example, for the radio beacon on the Nab Tower, is shown above. All the column headings are self-explanatory except 'No' and 'Mode'.

All the beacons in the world have an individual number, so '33' refers to the Nab Tower. An 'A' prefix would indicate that the number was that of an aerobeacon.

The designation 'A2A' in the 'Mode' column refers to the type of signal emitted by the beacon.

RDF RECEIVERS

As with most things you get what you pay for when you buy an RDF receiver. You will have to draw your own conclusions about value for money and what you want to spend, but there are one or two things to look out for when choosing.

Digital tuning Most modern sets now have this feature. It is certainly very useful to know beyond doubt that, although you may not have heard it yet, your set is tuned to receive the correct beacon.

Aerials with integral compasses Many RDF sets are permanently installed by the chart table, but have

No	Name	Ident		Range	Seq	Mode	Fog	Clear
77	Smith's Knoll Lt V	SK	· · · — · — ·	50	1	A2A	Cont	Cont
721	Goeree Lt	GR	— — · · — ·	50	2	A2A	Cont	Cont
85	Dudgeon Lt V	LV	· — · · · · · —	50	3	A2A	Cont	Cont
73	Outer Gabbard Lt V	GA	— — · · —	50	4	A2A	Cont	Cont
81	Cromer	CM	— · — · · — · —	50	5	A2A	Cont	Cont
709	N Hinder Lt V	NR	— · · — · — ·	50	6	A2A	Cont	Cont

BEACON SEQUENCE NUMBERS Commence transmission at the following minutes past the hour:

1 00 06 12 18 24 30 36 42 48 54	**2** 01 07 13 19 25 31 37 43 49 55	**3** 02 08 14 20 26 32 38 44 50 56
4 03 09 15 21 27 33 39 45 51 57	**5** 04 10 16 22 28 34 40 46 52 58	**6** 05 11 17 23 29 35 41 47 53 59

a portable, directional aerial with a compass attached. If this is so you want a good long lead, and a pair of headphones similarly equipped so that you can still 'listen in' while your head is outside the companionway. If you try to use a magnetic compass down below among the chart table instruments and close to the engine you are asking for poor results.

Smaller portable sets can be carried anywhere you like; the compass and aerial are integral and you move the whole set to get the bearing.

BFO A BFO control (Beat Frequency Oscillator) amplifies a normally quiet part of a radio beam so that you are hearing a tone all the time the station is transmitting. So long as you can hear the 'ident' (the morse identification letters) over the noise this is really useful because taking the null of a signal with the BFO switched on is very easy to do. If the BFO does mask out the ident then you just turn it off while you are identifying the station and then switch it on again to look for your null.

The Nab Tower beacon information includes a column headed 'Mode'. This refers to the type of radio signal being generated at the station. In some cases the signal may not be suitable for use with your BFO control, but the best practical advice I can give is to try the BFO switched on and switched off, and see which is better!

WHAT DO YOU HEAR?

When you tune in to a beacon, you will hear the ident signal transmitted at a sensible speed three times, followed by a long dash. At the end of the dash there is one further ident, after which the next signal in the group starts up. If the beacon is continuous, the signal is repeated.

Your job is to find the direction of the null. Even with the most sophisticated sets the null doesn't happen as crisply as you would hope, and often it seems to stretch over 20 or 30 degrees. If this is the case, cock your ears and 'sweep' from one side of the null to the other, homing in on it all the time. In the end you'll probably get it down to 10 or 15 degrees. So long as you can identify each side of the null, you can tell where it is by averaging the two sides out. Practice helps a lot.

Some sets have a small meter indicating signal strength, and these are a great help when looking for a null. The only trouble is that, in order to read the meter, you need to see the set while rotating the aerial. This means that you may create deviation

▽ The centre of the 'null valley' is the bearing of the beacon. In practice it is impossible to hear the centre, and you have to take an average between the points on each side where the signal becomes inaudible.

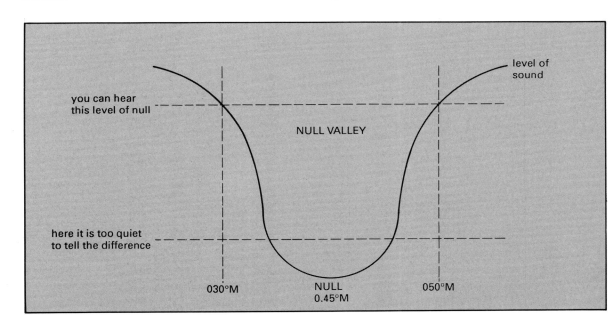

problems in your aerial compass by not being able to carry the aerial away from the chart table. Obviously this is not a problem with a portable set.

SOURCES OF INACCURACY

The skywave effect   Half an hour either side of sunrise or sunset RDF is almost useless because of disturbances to the nature of parts of the atmosphere. There is nothing you can do about this except avoid using the equipment at such times.

Half convergency   When you are operating on a beacon at a considerable distance from you, then great circle effects may become a factor. The radio signal, being a natural thing that has not heard of the Mercator projection, follows a great circle. The almanacs contain tables for handling this, but for most coastal work it need not be considered.

Quadrantal error   Radio waves are bent by certain parts of a vessel and this can make for a lot of inaccuracy in RDF results. Any error thus caused is called quadrantal error.

▽ You use an RDF receiver much like a handbearing compass, and must avoid operating it near metal fittings that might cause compass deviation or interference with the radio signal. For these reasons it works best out on deck.

▽ Lashing the guardrails with twine breaks the electrical ring round the boat and may greatly improve RDF reception.

Rigging is a prime sinner here, and guardrails. If an insulator is installed in the backstay and the guardrails have one end attached by lanyards, instead of rigging screws, then the 'basket' effect is broken and matters improve considerably. (You have also gained the facility to knife your guardrails in an emergency.) If you make these arrangements and you have the sort of set (or aerial) that can be carried up on deck then you have virtually beaten quadrantal error.

If you can't do this, then you must tabulate the error. You do this by placing the yacht within sight of a beacon, fixing your position by other means so that you know how the beacon should bear, and then taking a series of radio bearings on different headings. The difference between these and the real bearing is the quadrantal error and is noted on a curve like a deviation curve. Unlike the Deviation curve though, which varies with ship's head, the table of quadrantal error varies with the relative bearing of the beacon from the ship.

Compass deviation   Deviation is not normally too much of a problem for a headbearing compass because it is possible to take the compass to a part of the vessel where there is not much magnetically active material. You need to consider the same thing when using a movable RDF set (or a movable aerial). It is a matter of common sense. If you are forced by circumstances to use the beast on the chart table, then you'll have to include its compass errors in your 'swing' for quadrantal error and then make sure that you always use it in the same place.

It's very much simpler to buy a set or aerial that you can carry to a good place on board.

8 Shaping a Course

If you are sailing on a tideless sea with no currents, plotting a course to steer from one place to another is very easy indeed, and requires no elaboration here except a reminder that even in such ideal circumstances the boat will still make leeway.

COMPENSATING FOR LEEWAY

You will recall that when you are plotting leeway as part of an *estimated position* you simply draw in the 'course steered' a few degrees *downwind* of the course indicated on the compass.

If you are compensating for leeway when working up a *course to steer*, you should order the course a number of degrees *upwind* of what it would be with no leeway.

As before, the easy way to be sure of getting this right is to draw in the wind direction on the chart, place the plotter on the course to steer, and then imagine what you will do with the boat to compensate for leeway. Obviously, you will steer a few degrees to windward of the course, so rotate the plotter in that direction, and that is your course, duly compensated for leeway.

☞ **Rotate the plotter upwind to give a course to steer.**

SHAPING A COURSE ACROSS A TIDAL STREAM

Outside isolated tideless seas such as the Mediterranean, most courses have to be shaped with reference to tidal streams of one sort or another. If your course crosses a tidal stream it may have a dramatic effect on the accuracy of your landfall. You need to be able to predict such effects and, if necessary, compensate for them.

Short courses

Because a vector diagram for cross-tide navigation is only a diagrammatic representation of what is going on, it saves time and trouble to plot the picture of any short journey as a one-hour run. If you have done your sums correctly your boat will be sliding crabwise along the track between your departure and your destination. Within, or just outside the hour for which you have plotted, you will slide onto any object which is on the track, so it doesn't matter exactly how far it is to your destination. Here is the blow-by-blow technique for a one hour tidal vector diagram:

1 Plot the line joining your departure point (A) and your destination (B). This is going to be your *track* and is marked with a double arrow. It is a good idea to extend it a little way beyond B.

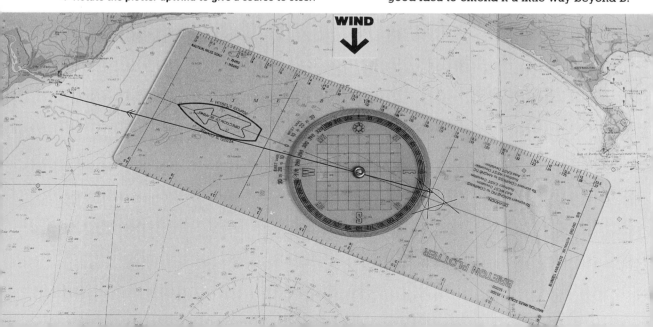

If the chart is too small to allow a full hour's diagram, then you can divide all the values by two. Because the vector triangle is only a construction drawing, this will make no difference to the results. The boat will still slide down the track.

The turn of the tide

If you envisage a two-hour passage across a strong tide in the process of turning, you have two choices open to you. You can compensate for each hour of tide in turn, like this:

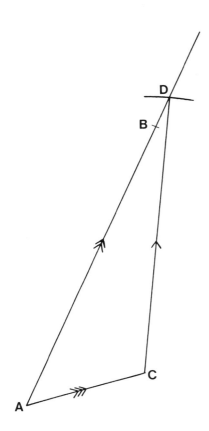

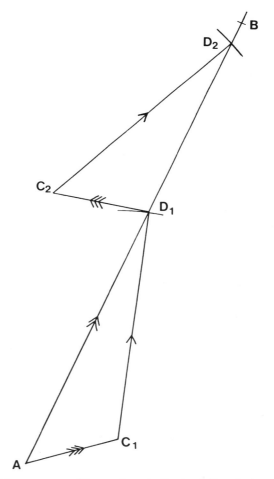

2 Draw in your *tide vector* from A to C, using the information extracted from the tidal stream atlas or the chart diamonds. Because you are drawing a one-hour diagram, one knot equals one mile on the chart. Note that the vector line has a triple arrow.

3 Set your dividers to represent the number of miles you expect to sail in one hour. Place one point at C, the end of the tide vector, and with the other point scribe across the track line, making a mark at D.

4 The line C to D is the course to steer. Correct this for leeway, plot it and advise the helmsman. Note that the course to steer has a single arrow.

If your destination is a little outside the 'triangle', the system works just as well.

This way, you will stay close to the track line, but you will have to alter course at the halfway point. You will also sail twelve miles through the water to make good ten miles over the ground.

Alternatively, you can average the tides out by allowing for both hours 'at one end' like this:

wander from the track, and her route over the ground will look like this:

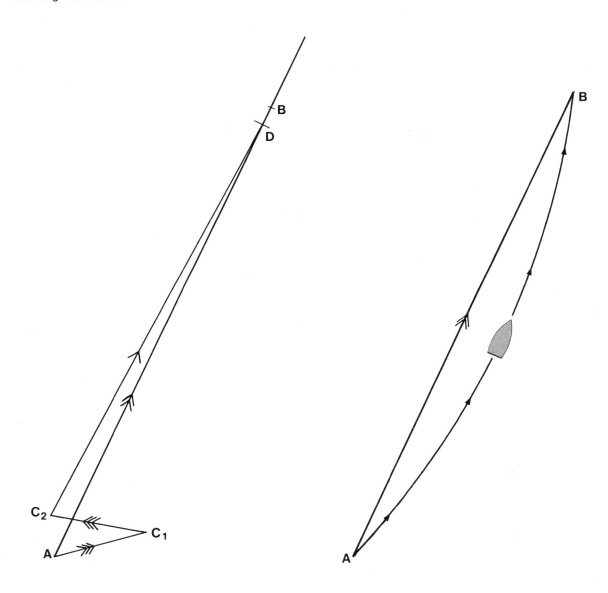

As you see, this boat has no alteration of course to make, and in order to reach B, she has only to sail a few yards over ten miles. *But* the tide will make her

It doesn't usually matter if you do 'wander' in this way, but it is important to know it is going to happen. If there were a danger to the right of the track, then you would have to lay off for each hour of tide individually. Otherwise, it is better to sail ten miles than twelve!

Long cross-tide passages

The best approach to cross-tide passages of more than one tide's duration is to estimate the number of hours you expect to take, and lay off all the tide you are expecting 'up front'. You then make an estimate of your boat's speed and multiply this by the number of hours you have worked on. Put one point of the dividers in the end of the composite tide line and cut the track with the other end as before.

Below is an illustration of what such a plot for a seven-hour passage might look like.

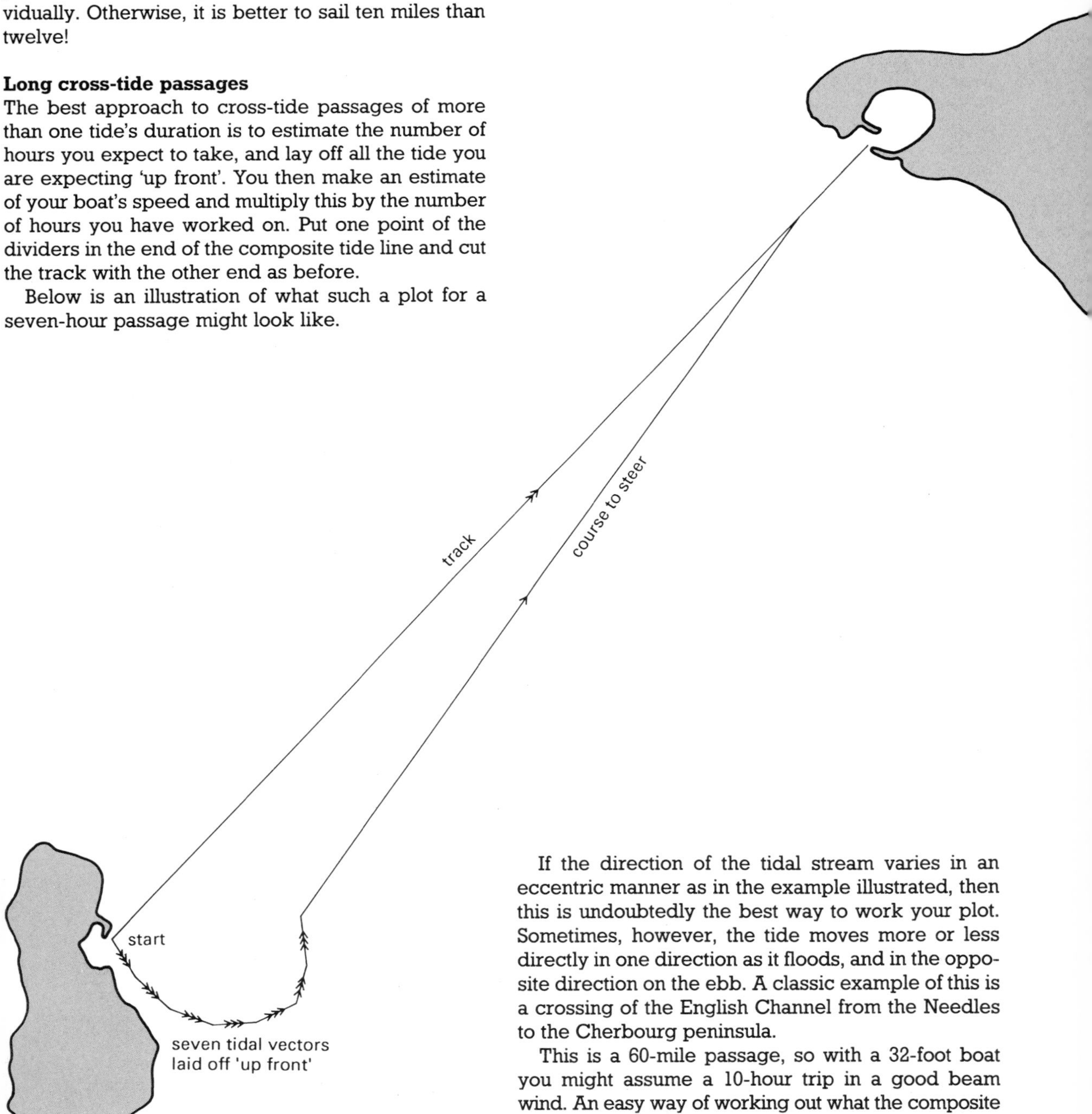

track

course to steer

start

seven tidal vectors
laid off 'up front'

If the direction of the tidal stream varies in an eccentric manner as in the example illustrated, then this is undoubtedly the best way to work your plot. Sometimes, however, the tide moves more or less directly in one direction as it floods, and in the opposite direction on the ebb. A classic example of this is a crossing of the English Channel from the Needles to the Cherbourg peninsula.

This is a 60-mile passage, so with a 32-foot boat you might assume a 10-hour trip in a good beam wind. An easy way of working out what the composite tide vector will be for that period is to add up all the east-going and all the west-going streams, then subtract the smaller from the greater and express the result as an aggregate, 'east', or 'west'.

This makes for a neat and readable plot. If, in contrast, you were trying to plot each hour of the tide on a chart of this scale, you would need a very sharp pencil and a good magnifying glass.

It could be said that to plot in this way is less than perfectly accurate, but remember that you are extremely unlikely to stay with this course all the way.

Sailing being what it is, you will not make exactly six knots for 10 hours. And however hard you try, when you have fixed your position at landfall you will probably have to lay off a new course anyway, so don't take too much trouble. Work up an overall vector and then keep up your EPs. You may have drifted anything up to 15 miles to one side of the track just before the tide turns, but if your speed holds more or less right, you'll slide back again in time to organise your final approach.

▷ **If you add all the east- and west-going streams on a cross-Channel passage and subtract one result from the other you will get an aggregate figure. You can use this to plot a single tidal vector for the trip (right).**

HOURS	WEST-GOING	EAST-GOING
1	2·6	
2	1·4	
3	—	—
4		0·8
5		1·8
6		2·2
7		2·8
8		2·0
9		0·3
10	—	—
TOTALS	4·0 W	9·9 E
AGGREGATE		5·9 EAST

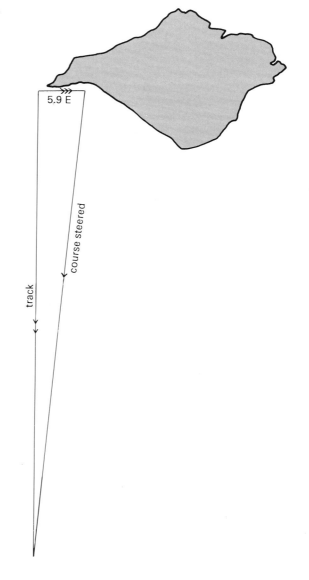

9 Lights, Buoys and Night Navigation

Night, at sea, runs officially between the hours of sunset and sunrise. Dead on sunset, all the lights come on (and so should yours). They stay on until the Sun has reappeared from around the back of the Earth.

Navigating at night is, in many ways, easier than daytime work, because although you may not be able to see as much, there is no difficulty whatever about identifying what you *can* see. The general features of the land have disappeared, leaving only the unambiguous pinpoint lights of the salient navigation marks. You can look at the chart and decide whether an inshore area is well enough lit to be able to navigate safely. If it is, then you have no problems at all. If you feel that it is not, then you can exercise your options and keep clear until daylight, or go somewhere else.

Dawn, and the few hours immediately following it, is probably the easiest time of all for the navigator. As the light grows you can see not only the lights of the identifying buoys and lighthouses, but also the features of the land. For this reason dawn landfalls have long been preferred by experienced navigators. At dawn you enjoy the best of both worlds.

LIGHTS AND BUOYS

For the purposes of this chapter it is assumed that you have a basic knowledge and understanding of the IALA (International Association of Lighthouse

A port-hand 'can' buoy (left) and a starboard-hand 'cone' buoy (right).

Authorities) system of buoyage which is in operation throughout British waters. As a revision, the system is illustrated below.

You will recall that, logically enough, the red and green port-hand and starboard-hand markers are lit with red or green lights, whose characteristics appear on the chart. Similarly, yellow special marks have yellow lights. What is less obvious is the logic of the system of white lights to be found on the Cardinal marks, isolated danger marks, and safe water marks.

Isolated danger marks flash in groups of two. They have two balls in their topmark. A safe water mark has a single ball topmark and its light produces a single long flash.

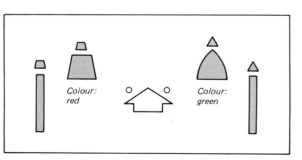

Port and starboard buoys and beacons.

Isolated dangers, safe water marks and special marks.

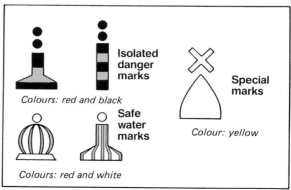

The system for the arrangement of lights on Cardinal marks is one of pure genius. The illustration opposite shows the four types of Cardinal buoy dispersed around a hazard with their light characteristics alongside them. If you imagine a clock face superimposed on them, you can see that three o'clock is over the East Cardinal, which emits three quick flashes – Q(3) – or three very quick flashes – VQ(3).

Six o'clock covers the South Cardinal whose rhythm is either VQ(6) plus one long flash – LFl – or Q(6) + LFl. The long flash serves to distinguish it from the West Cardinal (which has nine flashes) if the buoys are dipping below the waves.

Nine o'clock sits over the West Cardinal which flashes VQ(9) or Q(9), and 12 o'clock corresponds to the North Cardinal which, instead of flashing 12 times, simply never stops. It flashes continuously VQ or Q.

You may also have noticed that the points on the topmarks of Cardinal buoys indicate the position of the black colour. On the North Cardinal they point up, indicating that the buoy is black at the top. The pointers indicate black top and bottom on the East Cardinal, while on the West Cardinal they point firmly to the buoy's waistline. Both pointers aim down on the South Cardinal, towards the black base.

⇨ **A typical North Cardinal buoy.**

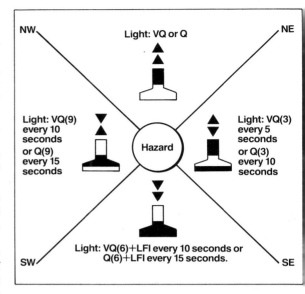

LIGHTHOUSES

Like all other lit navigation marks, lighthouses are shown on the chart with a magenta flash alongside. The name of the light is shown, and its light characteristics. The *nominal range* of the light is shown in *miles* (capital M) and the height of the *lantern* above MHWS indicated in *metres* (small m). The nominal range of a light is the distance from which its light can be seen in perfect visibility, irrespective of the height of the observer's eye above sea level, or the Earth's curvature.

Details of the symbols for the different characteristics of lighthouses can all be found in the booklet known as chart 5011, *Chart Symbols and Abbreviations*.

Lighthouses as a source of position lines
There are many more ways of taking a position line from a lighthouse than by simply looking at it over your handbearing compass. Here are some of them:
Coloured sectors Very often the arc of a lighthouse will have coloured sectors that indicate a particular danger, or pick out a channel. The detailed chart of the area (or the list of lights in the almanac) will tell you what angles the various sectors cover. When you pass from one to another, you have a position line (PL).

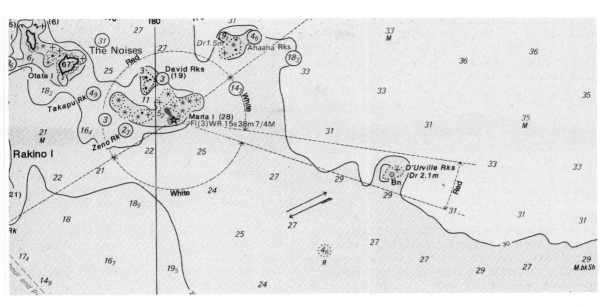

⌒ The red sectors of this lighthouse indicate dangerous rocks on the approach to Auckland, New Zealand.

Intensifying sectors   In some cases a light will show extra bright in a defined sector. In practice it is very easy to make out the intensification, so you know when you 'cross the line'.

Extra lights   Where there is a particular danger in the vicinity of a lighthouse there will sometimes be an auxiliary light shining in the sector that covers the dangers. The main light shines on all round. The cut-off point of the auxiliary light will give you an excellent position line.

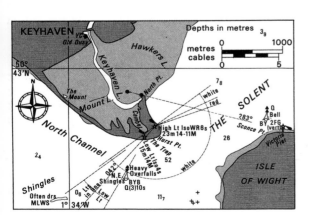

Rising and dipping distances

The powerful light from a lighthouse will not fade out as you sail away from it. Instead, because of the curvature of the Earth, it disappears below the horizon. If you know the height of the lighthouse, which is on the chart, and the height of your own eye, which you can usefully estimate, you can enter the 'Rising and Dipping' table in the almanac and read off your distance from the light.

On a calm, clear night this gives a surprisingly accurate result, but as the waves build up, particularly if you are in a small boat, it will be difficult to tell in the darkness what is horizon and what is wave. If this is the case, the best thing to do is clip on and go and stand by the mast. Your height of eye will be increased by two metres or so and everything will become much clearer.

When identifying lights, standing up is a very good policy at all times. It is easy to assume that a steady light is flashing because it is appearing intermittently from behind the waves.

◊ The additional low light on this lighthouse (to the left of the main arc) provides three position lines: one at each edge of its arc, and one in the centre, where it aligns with the main light to form a leading line.

loom of
powerful
distant
light

light dips as boat
sails over its horizon

⟿ As you sail over the horizon from a lighthouse, its light blinks out, or 'dips' (right). But a powerful light may still be visible by its loom (centre).

Looms

A powerful lighthouse on a clear night can usually be seen when it is still below the horizon because of its *loom*. This is the effect created by the light sweeping round and reflecting off a million water and dust particles in the atmosphere. Sometimes it is possible to see looms at a great distance: it is not unknown for the loom of St Catherine's Point light, on the southern tip of the Isle of Wight, to be visible from Barfleur 55 miles away.

You can take a rough bearing on a loom, but don't expect it to be very accurate.

OIL RIGS

In the last few years oil drilling platforms and pumping stations have become a feature of the seascape, particularly around nothern waters. These are generally brightly lit, and if they are burning off they can be seen at vast distances.

Oil platforms are an excellent aid to navigation, but some are frequently moved around. If you are going to make use of them, it is vital that your charts are kept right up to date, and that you listen out for the Navigation Warnings issued regularly by Coast Radio Stations.

UNOFFICIAL AIDS TO NIGHT NAVIGATION

All sorts of items not officially marked on the chart are lit at night, and if you are confident of their identity and position (and can plot them on the chart), there

is no reason not to use them. The quality varies from vague localities such as the end of a seaside town, to precise points like the floodlit facade of the 'Pilchard's Rest'.

Railway tunnels are marked on the chart, and if you see a train disappearing into one, grab a bearing on it quickly.

The arc lights over a dock are often far brighter than the single fixed light on the pier head, so think creatively about what you are actually seeing. But whatever you do *don't force things to fit*. Unless you are certain of the position of the 'Pilchard's Rest', don't use it!

▽ If you know the area, the illuminated facade of the Albion Hotel at Freshwater Bay could be a very useful landmark at night. But if you are simply looking for the 'HOTEL (conspic)' marked on the chart you may pick the wrong building, and you could be in trouble.

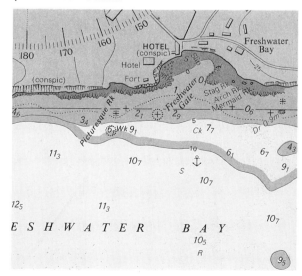

DANGERS IN THE DARK

The main danger involved with night navigation is that of hitting unlit objects, or even lit ones. Because you are seeing a flashing buoy only intermittently it is all to easy to become disorientated about scale and cross-sets and before you know where you are, there is a loud clang! Be careful.

Unlit objects fall into two categories: charted and uncharted.

If a buoy, or a post, is indicated on the chart as unlit then you need to exercise extreme care to keep well clear of it. You may do this by either giving it a very wide berth or, if you have to pass close to it, by using a clearing bearing of some sort to make sure you don't hit it.

As a last resort you can post an extra look-out, but look-outs alone on the foredeck at night tend to gather wool, and only come to their senses when they hear the clang. 'Unlit buoy under the bow skip!' 'Thanks very much . . .'

Uncharted unlit objects are usually found in the vicinity of the shore. Nobody can allow for the remote possibility that there may be a packing case or oil drum adrift in deep water, but when you are on the coast, *look out*. There may be lobster pots along the shoreline. In harbours the moorings, moored pieces of pipeline, unlit mussel rafts in Spain and all manner of floating hazards lie in wait for the unwary. If you fall foul of them there is only yourself to blame.

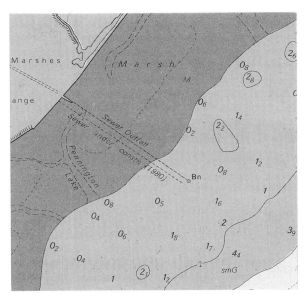

▷ **Keep a good look-out for unlit buoys and beacons. Shape your course to give them a wide berth, and stay alert as you approach. A modest post or buoy can make an impressive hole in a small fibreglass boat . . .**

Think twice before entering a strange harbour in the dark. It may look fine on the chart, but unless you have positive information that the entry and fairways will be completely clear, heave-to outside and wait for daylight.

10 Pilotage

As an offshore navigator, much of your time is spent guiding your vessel from one place to another with a good deal of water around you, and you use suitably large-scale navigation methods.

When you arrive in a strange harbour, or have to negotiate a group of close-packed offshore shoals or other dangers, then many of the usual techniques are either too slow and cumbersome, or do not give the incisive accuracy which you need. In these situations you must resort to the various practices which, taken together, are known as *pilotage*.

The essence of good pilotage is to work your way through the dangers on a sequence of positive, straight tracks which will carry you clear. All the tracks must be well-defined and, since the gaps you are negotiating may be narrow and the currents strong, it is rarely enough to merely 'steer the course' to pass through in safety. Instead you must use one of a variety of techniques to stay on a planned track until you reach the point where you change to the next one.

You hardly ever fix your position when piloting. All you need to know is that you are safely on the track from one point of your route to the next. There usually isn't time for a fix anyway.

KEEPING ON THE LINE

There are two basic types of line that you will use when piloting, and the ways of defining both are generally the same.

- The *safe track*. This is a track leading through the dangerous places. You must not err from this line by more than a few metres on either side.
- The *clearing line*. You use a clearing line when there is a danger to one side of your course. If you cross the line, you risk hitting the danger.

▽ A safe track defines a route through a danger zone.

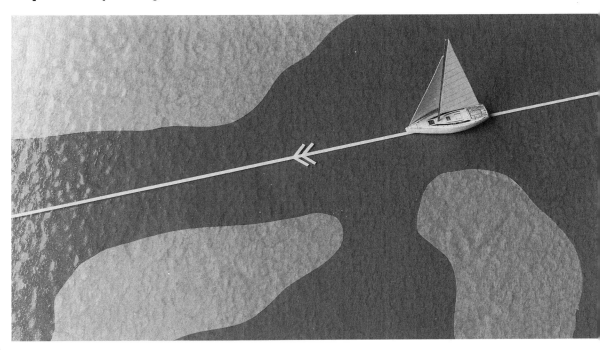

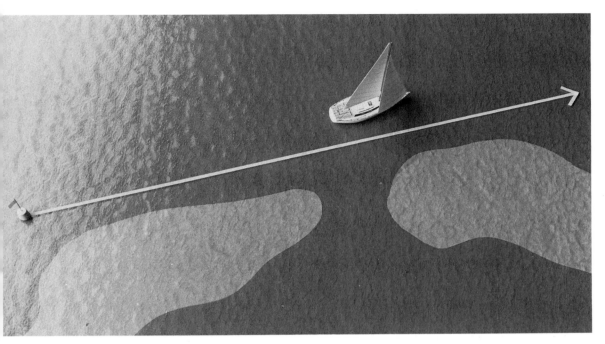

⌂ A clearing line defines the edge of a danger zone.

METHODS OF DEFINING A LINE

Whichever type of line you use, you need a foolproof way of defining it. The two most useful techniques are transits and bearings.

Transits

A transit of two objects lined up is the finest line definition. So long as you have identified the objects correctly and related them to the right ones on the chart, it is bulletproof. Transits come in various forms:

Leading marks. These need no explanation and are the best of all. The marks illustrated lead over the best water on the bar of the river.

◊ When the circular beacon is aligned with the V-shaped beacon you are on track to cross the river bar. The shapes are indicated on the chart (below).

Natural transits A natural transit is formed by two objects on the chart which, when placed one behind the other, will define the line you want.

↶ **Aligning two identifiable piles will give an excellent position line.**

Uncharted transits If the best 'line' you can produce is a bearing on, say, the next buoy, then if you transit the buoy with any fixed object behind it as soon as you are on the right line, you will stay on the correct bearing regardless of cross-set. This is an important technique when piloting up a twisting buoyed channel.

Lit transits Many leading lines are lit during the hours of darkness. Once again, for night pilotage these are the best lines you can find.

Bearings

Bearings are certainly the second-best method of defining a line or a track. They are subject to all the usual inaccuracies inherent in the magnetic compass, such as untabulated deviation (produced by the navigator's battery-operated hearing aid, perhaps?) and the compass card swinging in rough water, but if you cannot find a transit, bearings may be the best thing you've got. Here are some of the ways in which you can use bearings:

Light sectors These are often the most accurate bearing lines of all. The edge of a lighthouse sector is specified on the chart and is easily spotted in practice. As the light changes colour, you know how it bears.

Headings If you are steering a course from one mark to the next, you are running up the safe track defined by the bearing of the mark ahead. The problem is to keep the bearing constant.

Because the object is ahead of you, try to transit it as described. If you cannot do this because its only background is the horizon, then you should use the

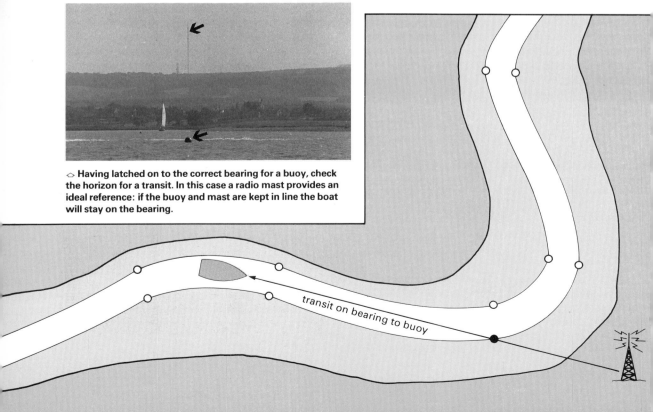

↶ **Having latched on to the correct bearing for a buoy, check the horizon for a transit. In this case a radio mast provides an ideal reference: if the buoy and mast are kept in line the boat will stay on the bearing.**

transit on bearing to buoy

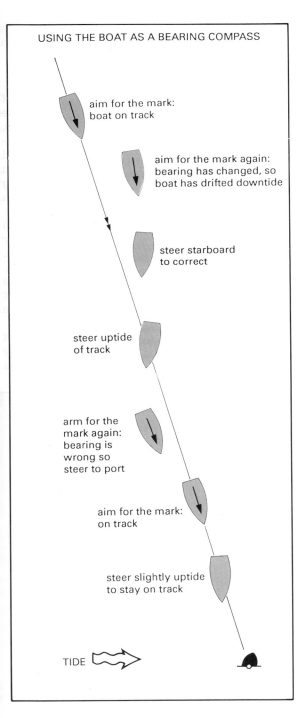

USING THE BOAT AS A BEARING COMPASS

aim for the mark:
boat on track

aim for the mark again:
bearing has changed, so
boat has drifted downtide

steer starboard
to correct

steer uptide
of track

arm for the
mark again:
bearing is
wrong so
steer to port

aim for the mark:
on track

steer slightly uptide
to stay on track

TIDE

whole boat as a bearing compass. Note the heading all the time as you steer for the mark. If it begins to alter you are drifting off track, so steer back onto your intended track and aim for the mark again to check the bearing. With practice you will be able to steer down the track with a fair degree of accuracy, compensating for cross-set and leeway while checking your bearing by occasionally aiming your boat at the mark.

Back bearings An easier way to stay on a single bearing is to look out for an object astern of you when you are on the line, and then keep its bearing constant. You may be able to pre-plan this by prior reference to the chart, or you may have to rely on observation at the time. If you go for the latter, the situation is much the same as when you transit a buoy with its background at the beginning of a 'leg'. If you don't do it straight away, you may be off the track by the time you get sorted out, and then you will run up the wrong line. As soon as you hit the course for the next mark, pick up a back bearing if you are going to need one.

◊ **Using the boat as a bearing compass (see text).**

▽ **Taking a back bearing on a lighthouse.**

The technique of running a back bearing is quite simple. Keep looking through your compass at the same bearing and if you find that you are no longer looking at your decided object, but to the left or the right of it, then turn the boat to bring yourself back onto the line.

↪ **Running a back bearing.**

Clearing Lines

So far we have discussed ways of staying *on* a line. In the case of a clearing line what you are trying to do is to steer *off* it, to one side in particular.

If you have defined the line with a transit, then you must keep the transit *open* on the safe side.

↪ **Using a clearing line defined by a transit.**

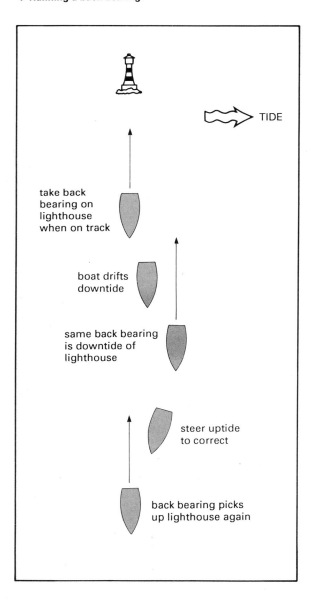

TIDE

take back
bearing on
lighthouse
when on track

boat drifts
downtide

same back bearing
is downtide of
lighthouse

steer uptide
to correct

back bearing picks
up lighthouse again

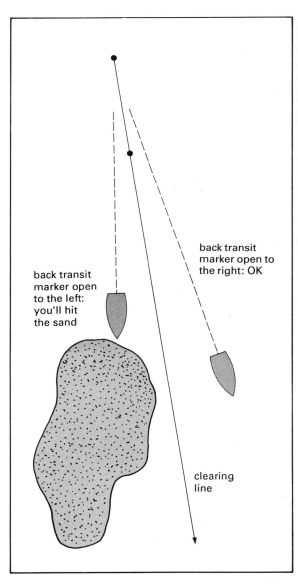

back transit
marker open to
the right: OK

back transit
marker open
to the left:
you'll hit
the sand

clearing
line

If your clearing line is defined by the bearing of an object, then you will have to ensure that the heading remains higher or lower than the clearing bearing, whichever is required. A simple sketch showing the situation (see below) will help you to work out which it should be.

▽ **Using a clearing line defined by a bearing.**

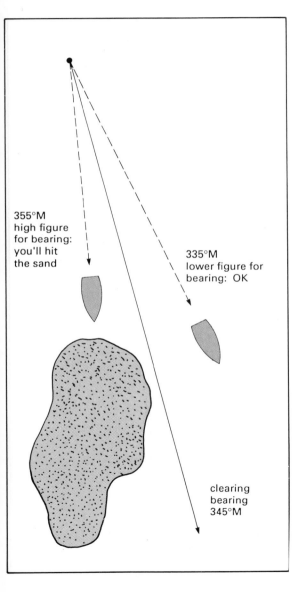

355°M high figure for bearing: you'll hit the sand

335°M lower figure for bearing: OK

clearing bearing 345°M

SAFE CORRIDORS

On many occasions the safe route between dangers on either side cannot be limited by a heading (towards a specific object), a leading transit or a back bearing, but it may be possible to 'cordon off' both sides of a *safe corridor* by lines which will clear the dangers.

You can define these lines by any method you choose. Ideally you find transits on both sides, but you may have to settle for a transit one side and a clearing bearing on the other, or even two clearing bearings.

▽ **Defining a safe corridor.**

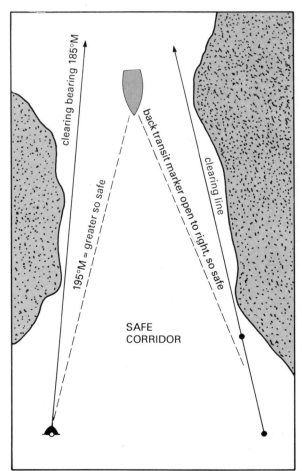

clearing bearing 185°M

back transit marker open to right, so safe

clearing line

195°M = greater so safe

SAFE CORRIDOR

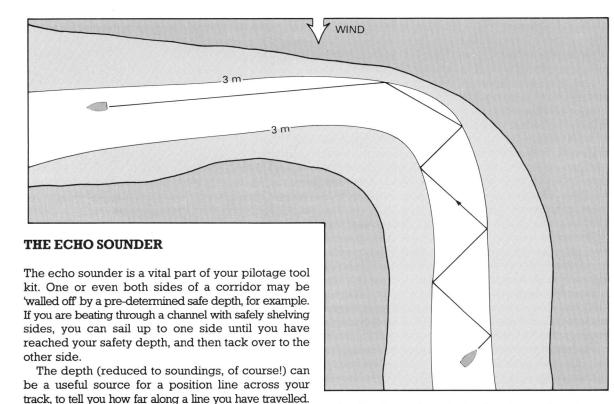

THE ECHO SOUNDER

The echo sounder is a vital part of your pilotage tool kit. One or even both sides of a corridor may be 'walled off' by a pre-determined safe depth, for example. If you are beating through a channel with safely shelving sides, you can sail up to one side until you have reached your safety depth, and then tack over to the other side.

The depth (reduced to soundings, of course!) can be a useful source for a position line across your track, to tell you how far along a line you have travelled. Often you can continue down a transit until the echo sounder indicates that you have reached a certain depth contour, after which it is safe for you to leave your line.

⏶ **Beating along a channel using the echo sounder to locate the contour line of the pre-determined safe depth.**

⏶ **Using a contour line to define the end of a tight channel marked by a transit.**

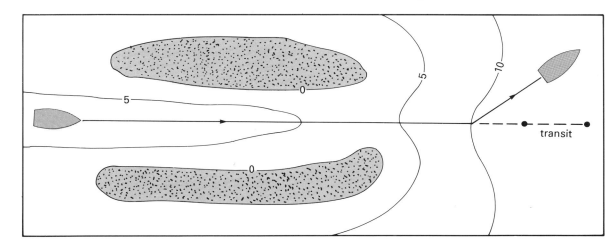

STEERING THROUGH GAPS OR CORRIDORS

Where an entry to a bay is blocked asymmetrically by shoals extending from each side it is still possible to judge by eye where the safe water is.

It is easy to judge the point halfway across *if you are approaching the gap at right angles*, but you will also find that you can mentally divide the entrance into three parts quite accurately.

If the chart shows that one of these imaginary dividing lines would lead safely in, you can often feel safe in passing through. It goes without saying, though, that if in doubt, DON'T!

Handrailing

If your passage lies between two objects (such as a visible steep-to rock to port and a shelving, ill-defined drying shoal to starboard) it is a good idea to keep close to the rock. Think of it as a handrail on a flight of stairs. If it is sufficiently steep-to to clear your keel and you stay five or ten metres off, there will be no doubt about whether or not you are avoiding the dangerous shoal to starboard.

TIDAL STREAM DIRECTION

If the stream is setting across your track, then your main problem in pilotage is to compensate for it. Its effects are obvious. What is not quite so obvious, on paper, is the effect of the tide in a narrow channel which is either right behind you, or dead against you.

It is good for morale to be swept towards your destination by the tide, but always remember that you have much less control over your boat's direction relative to the sea bottom – and the rocks – with the tide behind you.

With the tide foul, a slight alteration of course will result in a big sideways movement of the boat. This is useful if you are turning a sharp corner, or jinking up a narrow zig-zag channel. Don't forget, though, that you drift off your track extremely quickly in a foul current and, at night, this may not be immediately apparent.

Both fair and foul tides have their blessings and their vices. The important thing is to be aware of them.

INSTANT POSITION LINES

If you can possibly avoid it, you don't want to be messing about plotting magnetic position lines when you are piloting. You will have already noted a few salient bearings before you commit yourself, and what you want is to be able to check them quickly. It is surprising how many ways can be found to do this. Here are some examples, but you will think of others on the day.

- Object ahead: read the steering compass.
- Object astern: read the steering compass and add or subtract 180°.
- Object abeam (square across the mainsheet horse, companionway, cockpit coaming, etc.): read the steering compass and add or subtract 90 degrees. (Don't be afraid to deviate a little from your course to bring an object momentarily ahead, astern, or abeam. It's quicker than using your hand-bearing compass.)
- Objects 'opening': note the bearing on the chart at which daylight will appear between two objects.

⌂ Sight down the mainsheet track to bring an object directly abeam.

RECOGNISING OBJECTS

Most of the objects you are looking for are easy enough to recognise, but every now and again you'll come across an awkward one.

Even if you are certain you are seeing the correct thing it is always a wise precaution to check its bearing from a known point. If you are working a transit, look at its bearing to make sure that it is correct.

The best way to pick out an elusive buoy or shore marker is to find a very conspicuous, high, charted object that is near the line between you and the position of the missing mark. Draw a line on the chart joining the conspicuous object with the mark, and check its bearing from seaward. You now have a transit. Steer your boat to a place where the conspicuous object is on the transit bearing, and your mark must be just underneath it. Get out the binoculars and spot it.

▷ **Finding the buoy marked on the chart below is made easier by drawing a transit line from the buoy to the conspicuous tower on shore, and noting its bearing from the sea. When you reach the bearing the buoy should be directly in line with the tower (right).**

THE PILOTAGE PLAN

It is a mistake to think that you will be able to work through a pilotage operation by 'thinking on your feet'. Unless the passage is unusually straightforward, things will tend to run away from you and you will end up bobbing up and down the companionway from chart table to look-out like a Jack-in-the-box, until you slide to a quiet halt on the waiting mud. The way to avoid this ignominy is to organise a *pilotage plan* well in advance.

You should study your detailed charts and pilot books carefully and then make up a set of notes. It may well be that your pilot book will serve you up a complete pilotage plan on a plate. Even if it does, remember that it is only there to augment the chart. If it doesn't, you are going to have to write your own.

The actual system you use for noting things down will be up to you, but it really pays to mark all courses, distances, bearings and course alterations. You won't have time to use your plotting instruments as you zoom up the sluice with the tide behind you. If all the data is to hand, either drawn on the chart, or presented in a list, then you are halfway to success.

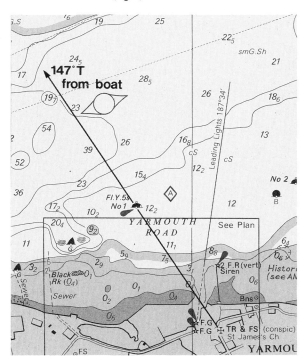

While you are operating your plan it is best to keep your chart (suitably folded) and your notes by you in the cockpit. Get someone else to steer, so that you are free to take bearings and keep your eye on the overall picture.

Know the tide

It is a good idea to have worked out the height of tide for the period you will be piloting. It may not be relevant to your safe passage according to plan, but if things go awry you may find yourself navigating in 'thinner' water than you intended and then you'll be glad that you worked out the tide height in advance.

Depending upon the conditions, your boat and the type of harbour you are dealing with, you may decide that a particular stage of tide is favourable for your entry.

Suppose that there is no question about where the navigable channel lies, but its depth is in doubt. Is there going to be enough water for you? In this case you would be well advised to enter one and a half hours before high water. This would give you a good chance of floating in, but if you found bad news waiting in the form of the mud bank you were afraid of, then there will be enough tide still rising to float you off for your retreat.

On the other hand , if you are navigating up an ill-marked Brittany river with a nine-metre rise and fall of tide where you risk missing the channel and going aground, the ideal time would be soon after low water, with most of the drying banks exposed for all to see and lots of tide to come in, just in case . . .

THE LAST RESORT

Finally, never enter shoaling water without an anchor handy – and make sure its cable is securely attached to the boat! You may run out of wind, your engine may die, or you may just find yourself disorientated and want to stop.

Anchoring is free, and it's not just for stopping overnight in secluded bays; it is also your last line of defence.

11 Passage Planning

The success or failure of a passage depends, more than anything else, on how well it has been planned. If you have thought carefully about the possible combinations of tide, wind and weather, then your passage will be easy on the ship and her crew. You will arrive in good spirits and people will enjoy sailing with you, although they may not know the secret of your success. The man who fails to plan his passages properly is dogged by 'bad luck' all the way. He is a passive victim of the tides and the changing wind, rather than a skipper for whom all things appear to work together.

▽ **Good passage planning is the secret of satisfying, enjoyable sailing. Neglect it and you could have a mutiny on your hands.**

The factors you should take into account when preparing for a passage will depend on the circumstances. Here are some of the more important things that you should consider.

CHARTS AND DISTANCES

Once you have decided where you want to go, you should make sure you have all the charts you need to cover the passage and your arrival and departure. Spread out the passage chart and lay off the approximate distance to your destination. What will be your speed? Can you make the trip in one tide, two or more?

Study your charts, make sure they are up to date, and read the passage notes in your pilot books.

Viable alternatives

A destination is always more desirable if there are some good workable alternatives on either side of it. Have a good look to see if there are any, then check their entry requirements for such things as tidal clearance so that you can use them if you miss a tide, get fed up, cold or seasick, or if you are having a great sail and want to press on further.

Ports of refuge

If you have the slightest doubts about the weather make sure that, if possible, there is a port of refuge on the way to your destination. This may be one of your viable alternatives, or it may not, but you should take care to note whether it has tidal restrictions and if it is safe in all weathers. Many a port which is perfect in a south-westerly of any strength is a death trap in an easterly gale.

Range under power

Be aware of what your range is, and then make absolutely sure you have enough fuel on board to handle a windless passage, or a dismasting. It never pays to skimp on filling fuel tanks. You'll have to buy the stuff in the end and there is nothing more calculated to sap morale than sitting in front of a closed tidal gate watching the same lighthouse for six hours because you didn't have your fuel organised.

Point of no return

There is always a point on a passage from which it is quicker and easier to go on than to turn back. Knowing where this point is (and depending upon such things as tidal stream and wind direction it may be something other than the halfway mark) can be a useful safety control, particularly in an emergency brought about by gear failure, personal injury or illness.

Traffic Separation Zones

The Collision Regulations require that Traffic Separation Zones are either used with the flow of traffic, entered at a shallow angle, or crossed at right angles if a crossing cannot reasonably be avoided. If your passage takes you anywhere near one of these you should be sure to take this into account. Contravening the rules could have dire consequences.

Heavy concentrations of commercial shipping are always bad news for yachtsmen. If you have any choice in the matter, try to avoid them.

Pilotage plans

These should always be prepared in good time. If the plan refers to your destination then you may prefer to make it up while you are on passage but, whatever you decide, don't let it be a last-minute rush.

WEATHER

Before setting out on a passage of any length, you should have a clear overall picture of the weather pattern. The best way to achieve this is to listen to the shipping forecast for a few days prior to leaving, and to keep a check on the weather maps in a good newspaper. If you have done this it will be a lot easier to plot your own maps from the forecasts you receive on passage, and you will be in a far stronger position to make cruise strategy decisions.

Be flexible in your plan for a cruise. It is a grave mistake to decide, a month before leaving your base at Holyhead, that you are going to round Lands End and cruise the south-west coast. The wind may be set in the south for a week or more and no amount of careful planning can alleviate the discomfort of a 250-mile dead beat!

TIDE

If there is one thing more important when planning a passage than the weather forecast, it is the state of the tide.

Tidal streams

As soon as you have noted the distance to your destination the next thing to do is to open up the tidal stream atlas and see what can be done to extract every mile of benefit from the tide. It is particularly important to locate and plan for the *tidal gates*. These are places where the tide runs extra fast: prominent headlands, corners such as Dover, and sluices of the magnitude of the Race of Alderney where the stream reaches a good seven knots at times.

Gates like this must be open for you, and on the way you will need to work out your required speed carefully to make sure that they are. A good way to do this is to draw some concentric arcs of a circle spreading out from the gate with critical times noted on each one.

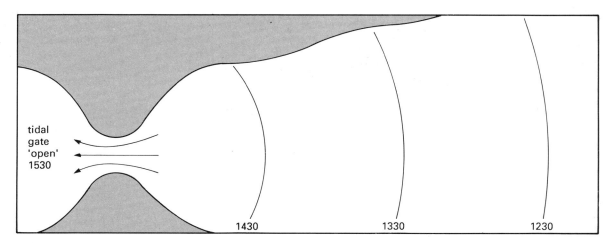

tidal
gate
'open'
1530

1430　　　　　1330　　　　　1230

⌂ **Drawing concentric arcs at defined distances from a tidal gate will help you check your progress and arrive at the ideal time.**

If you are late reaching a particular circle you must crack on, starting the engine if necessary, because if the gate shuts you are going to have a long, demoralising wait.

At the planning stage you should pencil in what the ship's time will be on the various pages of the tidal atlas, and also pencil in the time of high water at your Standard Port on the chart, if you are proposing to use the tidal diamonds. This makes looking ahead much easier and saves bookwork along the way.

If your passage is a cross-tide one such as a Channel crossing, make up a table of hourly east and west sets. This will help you work out the 'aggregate set' once you know how fast you will be going.

Tidal heights
While many ports are free of tidal height considerations, many are not. Your destination may have a difficult bar, or the depths inside may be controlled by a sill. Maybe you need to lock in or dry out, or perhaps you just want to enter a river you do not know near the top of a rising tide.

Any of these considerations make for a 'window' that will only open at certain times to let you in. You must know the earliest and latest times that the window will be off the latch and try to control your speed accordingly. Once again, concentric circles showing where you should be at each hour for a few hours before arrival are a great help.

Reduction to soundings
If your passage is to cross an area of shoal water such as the Thames Estuary, you will need a clear idea of the state of the tide throughout the trip. Work it out for each hour before you start. If things are becoming fraught on passage owing to weather, seasickness or just plain tiredness, you will bless yourself for your forethought.

OFFSHORE DANGERS

This is where close inspection of the chart pays off. Dangers may take many forms: an off-lying rock, a shoal over which the sea may break, a tide rip or an unlit buoy. They should all be considered and planned for *in good time*. Don't wait until you are nearly on top of the problem before having a frantic search on the chart for a clearing bearing.

DAY OR NIGHT

In Chapter 9 we looked at the desirability of a dawn landfall. If you want one, plan for it.

Sometimes it is expedient to enter a harbour at night. If this is the case it will pay you to have a bit of moonlight to alleviate the thick darkness. Keep an eye on what the moon is doing so that you can plan for this, or look up the times of moonrise and moonset in the almanac. Don't worry about the detailed corrections; all you need is a rough idea.

COURSES TO STEER

There is a tendency to do too much preparation of these. Remember that a sailing boat is an unpredictable beast. The wind may be less strong than you anticipated, slowing you down and throwing out your course and tidal stream calculations, or it could go round and stop you laying the course at all. What you need is a rough idea of direction so that when you arrive at your departure point you can give the helmsman some sort of a course. You can then see how the boat is performing and go and work out a proper one.

Waypoints
If you have a Decca, now is the time to decide which waypoints to use, and programme them in.

TACTICS

In a boat, the quickest and most comfortable route between two points is not always a straight line, even if you are not beating to windward. You need to think tactically about how to make best use of what is on offer in the way of wind and tide.

For example, if you are making landfall on a coast along which the tide runs hard, it will always pay to be a little uptide of the straight track to your destination.

This holds good regardless of wind direction. You can always allow the tide to carry you down, but to fight your way back up against it, particularly to windward, or when bearing away in a falling wind, is demoralising in the extreme.

If you are sailing on a coastal passage in a strong wind with a fair tide, you could well decide that it is worth losing a little of the benefit of that tide in order to sail closer inshore under the lee of the land. Your boat will sail faster in the smoother water and all hands will have a far happier time.

BEATING TO WINDWARD

If there is no tidal cross-set, the secret of successful beating to windward is to stay on the making tack. The wind is rarely dead 'on the nose' and, if it is, it doesn't usually stay there long. One tack or the other is generally favoured (see illustration) and if you are on that tack you are covering more ground towards your destination than you would on the other. So long as you stay on the favoured tack until you are dead downwind of your destination, you will not go wrong.

▱ **All other things being equal, try to stay on the favoured tack towards your destination.**

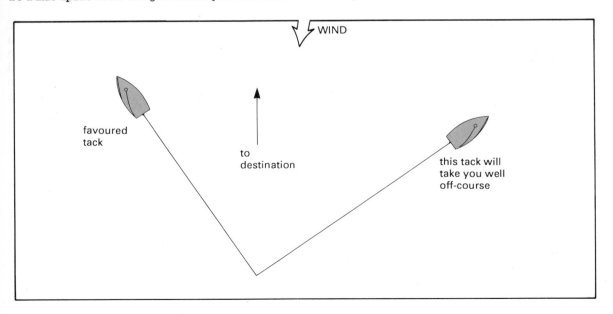

WIND

favoured
tack

to
destination

this tack will
take you well
off-course

If the wind shifts at any time you should reassess the situation and tack if necessary. A shift will either *free* you, or *head* you. If you are freed, you are clearly going to stay on the same tack, but if you are headed then you may well have ceased to be on the making tack, in which case you should go about and try the other one.

If the wind stays on the nose, then you should try and tack down a cone spreading out at about ten degrees on either side of the dead downwind line from your destination. This will keep you close enough to the direct course to take advantage of any windshifts in your favour, and not be 'knocked' much if the wind shifts 'against you'.

▽ **Tactical use of windshifts.**

▽ **Tacking down a cone towards your goal.**

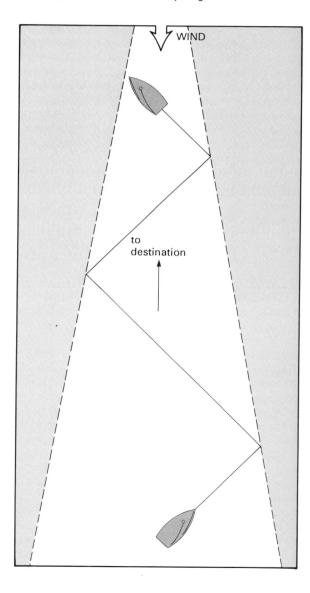

WIND   favoured tack

WINDSHIFT

wind veers –
favoured tack is
freed, so stay on it

WINDSHIFT

wind backs –
you are headed,
so go about to
try new tack

WIND

destination

WIND

to
destination

Anticipated windshifts

If you are expecting the wind to shift in a certain direction, you would be well advised to stand on further than the ten-degree cone in the direction of the shift so that, when it comes, you are well placed to take full advantage of it.

Example You are beating down-channel in a south-westerly with a forecast veer (clockwise windshift) to the north-west expected soon. In this case it would be wise to stand well to the northward on the port tack, then when the veer comes you may be able to 'lay your course'.

▽ By tacking south before an expected veer (top), boat A has left herself with nowhere to go when the veer comes. Boat B has tacked north (bottom), so when the wind veers she is freed and able to head straight down the Channel.

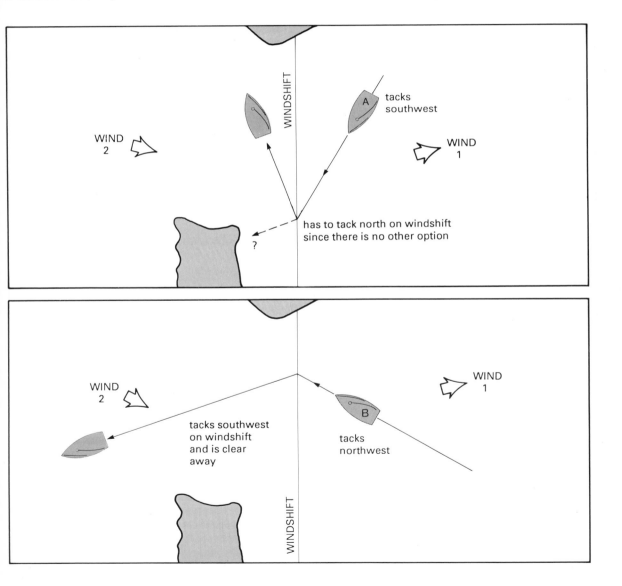

Beating in a cross tide

When you are sailing to windward your prime objective is to move your boat up towards the wind, for that is the general direction of your destination.

The lee bow effect   Keeping a cross tide on your lee bow, rather than your weather bow, will make a dramatic difference here as the lee-bowing tide will actually lift the boat to windward. The diagram shows the massive advantage to be gained by this tactic.

If the passage is a long one, during which the tide turns to run back the other way, and both boats in the diagram tack with the turn of the tide, boat B will be carried back to the rhumb line again but when she crosses tacks with boat A she will find herself far to leeward.

The reason for this is that a boat with the tide on the lee bow enjoys a freer apparent wind than a boat with the tide on the weather bow. This is because the lee-bowing boat experiences a wind component coming from the opposite direction to the tide, over her weather quarter. When this is added in to the apparent wind on the weather bow, it frees it a little. The boat with her weather bow to the tide suffers the opposite effect.

There is nearly always more than one way to make a passage. Look at the whole picture carefully; free your mind of the natural land-born tendency to go straight for your objective and bear in mind that you are on a rolling road whose movements you can predict with considerable accuracy.

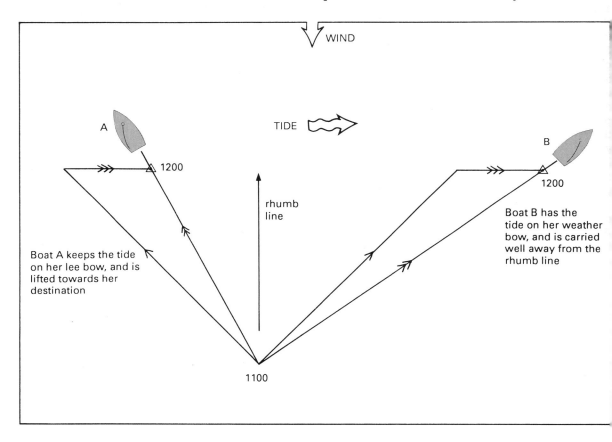

12 Practical Passagemaking

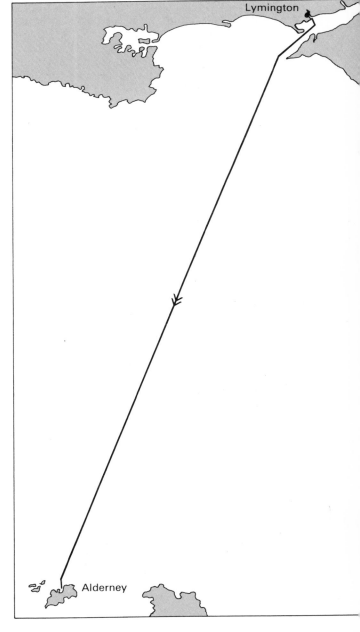

One of the greatest problems experienced by student navigators is deciding how much navigation to do, what sort to do, and when to do it. This final chapter is dedicated to the question of how you actually operate during an offshore passage.

The passage used as an illustration is a crossing from the south coast of England to the Channel Islands. The plan is to leave Lymington in the afternoon and take the ebb tide down to the Needles. Then, wind permitting, to make a night crossing to Alderney, arriving in time for breakfast. The wind looks like staying in the west at force four, and the forecast is for good visibility.

1 Make your passage plan. If you have not made the passage before, you will be hoping for a dawn landfall, so your projections of time and distance should work backwards and forwards from that point. This may not work out in practice, but it is as good a place as any to start from. Working back from the dawn landfall towards your departure from Lymington, you will discover no difficulties until you come to the initial sail down the West Solent from Lymington to the Needles. This is probably going to be a beat, so you will need to have the tide in your favour.

Dawn is at 0430 GMT and you want to be about 15 miles north of the big lights on Cap de la Hague and Alderney (your probable landfall) around that time. It is 45 miles to this area from the Needles so, if you expect to make five knots through the water, you need to be off the Needles nine hours before, or 1930 GMT. As it happens, the tide is ebbing westwards from 1600, so you have no problems.

2 Moving from Lymington to the Needles in good visibility is a question of pilotage. Refer to your pilotage plan and enjoy the sail.

3 When you arrive at the Needles, the first thing to do is to put the boat on an approximate course towards Alderney and *log your departure*.

◊ **The route from Lymington to Alderney.**

4 Once you are settled, trimmed and making a steady speed you can work up a proper course to steer. See how many hours the passage will take at this speed and refer to the table of east-going and west-going tide you made up as part of your passage plan (Chapter 11). Then shape your course and pass it up to the helmsman as soon as possible. It should only differ from your initial approximate heading by a few degrees, so you can consider that you have been steering it right from your departure point.

(Incidentally, *never* give the helmsman a course to steer without first looking along the bearing. You may have made a mistake. Perhaps you applied deviation the wrong way, maybe you have given him a reciprocal course, or possibly you are sending him into the path of a flying boat on its take-off run. The possibilities for a nonsense are endless, so make sure you haven't dropped a brick before you leave him to it.)

During the next hour, or so, it is worth discreetly watching your helmsman and how he is steering. Often disappointment awaits the navigator who assumes complete skill and honesty from the person at the tiller. Many boats on a reach try to drive upwind of the course and it takes experience to counteract this tendency. Watch your courses carefully and encourage your crew to report faithfully on their progress.

5 So long as the English coast and its lights are visible, keep up an hourly estimated position and confirm it by fixing. This will give you the opportunity of seeing if things are developing as you expected, and also provide a running check on your log, compass and Decca (if you have one).

6 Just before the land or the lights lose their clarity, or disappear, take a visual departure fix. This is the last truly confirmed position you can work back to until you reach the other side.

7 GO TO BED. Look after yourself. You'll be needed later; right now there is nothing vital to do so get some sleep. Before you go, though, you should instruct the watch on deck to note the course and the log reading every hour. If they have the inclination and ability they can keep the plot going by working up hourly estimated positions, but the important thing is regular log entries.

8 Rouse yourself out somewhere around mid-channel and work up the estimated position from the log entries, beginning at your departure fix. When you have done this, you might check it with an RDF or Decca fix and deduce your position by relating one to the other. Are they in reasonable agreement? They should be within a couple of miles of one another. If they are not, start looking for the reason why. If they are, shape a course from this fresh departure point. Given that your speed has remained constant and your tidal predictions were accurate, this new course should be much the same as your original one, but even if this is so the exercise is well worth the effort.

▽ **Be sure to get some sleep. If you stay up all night you'll be in no fit state to manage the landfall.**

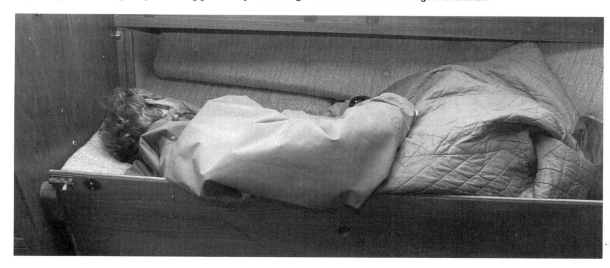